Standard Catal

Schwinn

Doug Mitchel

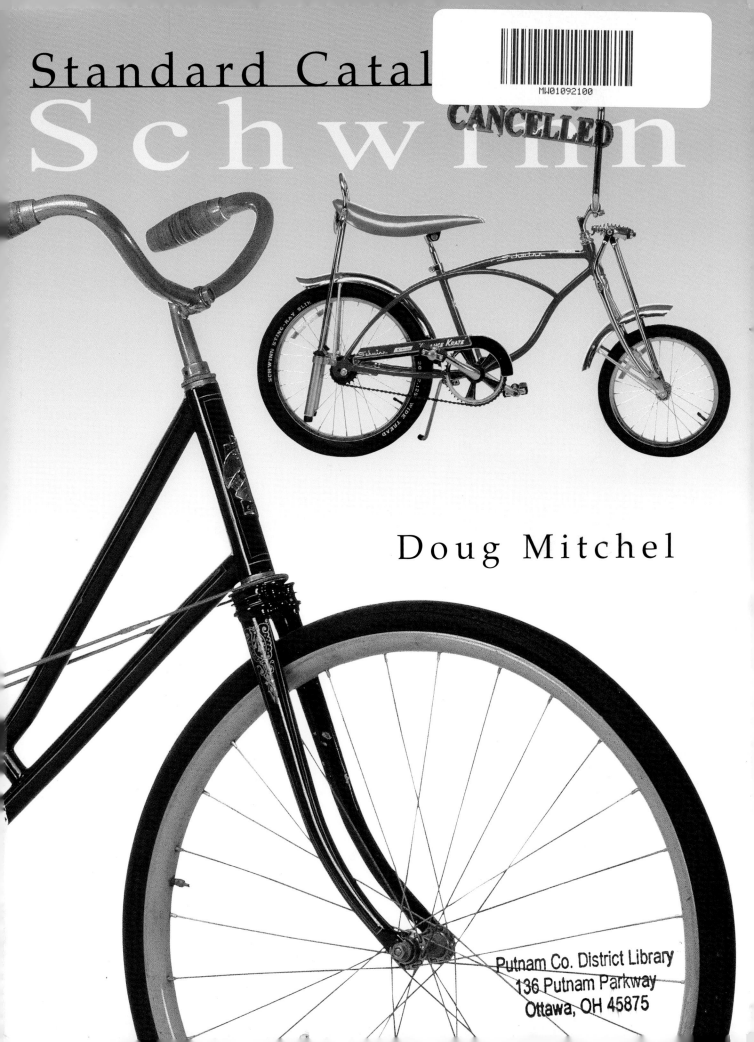

©2004 Doug Mitchel

Published by

kp books
An imprint of F+W Publications, Inc.

700 East State Street • Iola, WI 54990-0001
715-445-2214 • 888-457-2873

Our toll-free number to place an order or obtain
a free catalog is (800) 258-0929.

Library of Congress Catalog Number: 2004116645
ISBN: 0-87349-884-4

Designed by Gary Carle
Edited by Dan Shideler

Printed in the United States of America

Dedication

To Mary H., the love of my life.

Acknowledgments

Larry Anderson

Rex and Kathy Barrett

Rod and Marc Griffis, Blue Moon Bikes Ltd., Sycamore, IL

The Bill Figatner Collection

Jeff and Greg Hajduk at Barnard's Schwinn, Oak Park, IL

The Andy and Wendy McGann Collection

Michael Mitchell

The Matt Mutchler Collection

Ronn Pittman

Dale Walksler's Wheels Through Time Museum, Maggie Valley, NC

A very special thanks to the Bicycle Museum of America, New Bremen, OH,
for extending every courtesy and effort during my visit to their amazing collection.

Contents

Introduction

O dds are, if you mention the name "Schwinn" to anyone over 25 years of age, you will quickly be regaled with a story. It may be the one about a magical Christmas when a new 10-speed Continental was received, or how the kid down the street had a Stingray or Krate you always lusted after. Even stories about the earlier balloon-tire models make their appearance when the proper chord is struck. For many, extra chores around the house, or a few additional hours on the job, earned us the money we needed to bring our goal closer to reality. Cross-country rides, jumping over home-made ramps, or taking your first test ride in the snow are what Schwinn bicycles have meant to many of us.

As with many corporate success stories, the beginnings of the Schwinn bicycle history are humble. A young boy, eager to make his way in life, finds himself obsessed with the latest mechanical device, as well as being gifted with the talent and vision to bring his dream to reality. After years of learning the craft, he sets out to create a name for himself. Making the long journey from Germany to America, Ignaz Schwinn probably had other things on his mind besides how his dream would end up touching so many lives. Looking back, I'm sure that most victorious entrepreneurs are amazed how far their early dreams have taken them.

The story of Schwinn has its share of ups and downs, just as any venture might have. The fact that so many of us have been a part of the ride, though, makes it all the more personal and exciting!

The now-famous Schwinn bicycle company started innocently enough when Ignaz Schwinn was born on the first day of April in 1860. He was the second of seven children born to the family of meager means. The small town of Hardheim, Germany, located in the Province of Baden, was hardly a pinnacle of commerce. Ignaz's father's vocation as the owner of an organ and piano factory kept him away from home for much of the time. He died when Ignaz was 11, inspiring Ignaz to become a craftsman as his father had been.

This "family tandem" was built specially for the Schwinn family to enable Ignaz and his wife to ride with young Frank W. between them. On most tandems, the rider in front was in charge of steering. In this case, Ignaz was seated in the rear, but still had control over the bike's direction through the linked handlebars.

A small stipend supported Ignaz through primary and vocational school, after which he began his apprenticeship as a machinist. In a small town work was often not readily available, limiting Ignaz's opportunities in existing fields. As with many young boys, the new "high-wheel" bicycles drew his attention. The "Safety" bike being built in England was of particular interest to Ignaz. This new style of two-wheeled transport featured a pair of smaller-diameter wheels, thus keeping the rider much closer to the ground. The high-wheeled models had proven to be quite dangerous,

especially to beginning riders.

While work may have been scarce, Ignaz's talents proved to be almost limitless. His employer machined components for a bicycle manufacturer named Heinrich Kleyer, and this connection only helped to feed his desire. After a long day as an apprentice, he would spend hours each night in his living quarters above the machine shop dreaming and designing his own bicycle.

Fascinated with the Safety bicycle, he began to design his own version of the two-wheeled machine. Since technology was not easily

The basket between Dad and Mom was the perch for little Frank W. Schwinn.

accessible, his designs were based on existing and proven techniques.

Eighteen-eighty-eight saw the introduction of the pneumatic tire, and this innovation was sketched into his ground level plans. After finalizing his design, he showed his plans to Heinrich Kleyer. Impressed by his work, Heinrich hired Ignaz to design a German Safety bike. His talents would lead him to assist in the design and construction of a new factory for Heinrich Kleyer bicycles in 1889. This company would go on to become Adler Works of Germany and also produced motorcycles that carried the Adler badge from 1900 to 1957. Ignaz continued to prove his mettle and made great strides within the organization. A trip to the World's Fair in Chicago in 1891 would prove to be his jumping-off point in the United States. Ignaz was exposed to advances in technology and metallurgy that he may have missed in his home country. What had begun as a vocation soon became a calling. He decided to stay in Chicago.

His reputation as a designer and builder preceded him, and he was soon hired by Hill &

Moffat, manufacturers of the Fowler bicycle. This position was short-lived, and he next found himself under the employment of the International Manufacturing Company. His role as a designer of bicycles led to his assistance in planning for a new facility for the company. Unhappy with the way the company was managed, he left International's employ in 1894.

In 1895, Ignaz would make a fateful acquaintance. Adolf Frederick William Arnold was 11 years older than Ignaz and wore many hats. Besides being an investor, he was an executive of a meatpacking plant and the owner of Chicago's

The adult riders had one of these rather austere saddles to rest their haunches on.

Haymarket Produce Bank. As it so often had in his past, Ignaz's talent and ambition impressed Mr. Arnold. Not being one to pass a great opportunity, the entrepreneur formed an alliance with Ignaz that laid the foundation for the Arnold, Schwinn & Co.

With Arnold's financial backing and Ignaz's technical abilities, the company first set up shop just west of Chicago. The rented facility was located at the corner of Lake and Peoria and would be the first step towards their goals of producing high-quality bicycles at a profit.

The year they decided to join forces and begin building bicycles was hardly a boom period in the world. The two previous years were marred by financial distress and horrific labor woes. Nearly a million employees were involved in thousands of labor strikes involving over 25,000 different firms. Riots, violent confrontations, and executives being jailed were common during this period. In light of the current economic environment, it seemed that things could only get better.

In stark contrast to the condition of the country's labor status, however, the bicycle industry was booming. With 300 companies building bicycles and several hundred more making related components, things were never better. The Schwinn company catalog was filled with seven highly engineered, well-built machines. Bicycles ranged from simple men's and women's models to the five-place "Quint." A variety of frame sizes allowed customers to custom-build a unit that best fit their own frame. A tandem model named the "Combination" was ridden by Ignaz, his wife Helen and their first child, Frank W. Mounted between the two adult pillions was a third, child-sized seat. Racing customers could purchase the "World" Racer, which sold for $125 and weighed only 19 pounds. The racing models were also available with a variety of frame sizes and options.

Before the downturn in the bicycle market, two-thirds of the country's bicycles were built within a 150-mile radius of Chicago, the home of Schwinn.

Prices ranged anywhere from $40 to $120 each, and many people paid for their bikes over time. Nationwide production had reached nearly one million units, and seemed to know no bounds. With new buyers often waiting months for their new bicycles, it was the perfect time for the Arnold, Schwinn and Company to take the next step and incorporate.

In stark contrast to the condition of the country's labor status, however, the bicycle industry was booming. With 300 companies building bicycles and several hundred more making related components, things were never better.

While the main purpose of the firm was to build bicycles and their related parts, Ignaz found time to design and build one of the first electric cars in Chicago. His ride through the streets of Chicago caused quite a stir and was a harbinger of things to come.

Shortly before the next century made its entrance, the bicycle industry had fallen on hard times. After reaching a pinnacle over 1.2 million

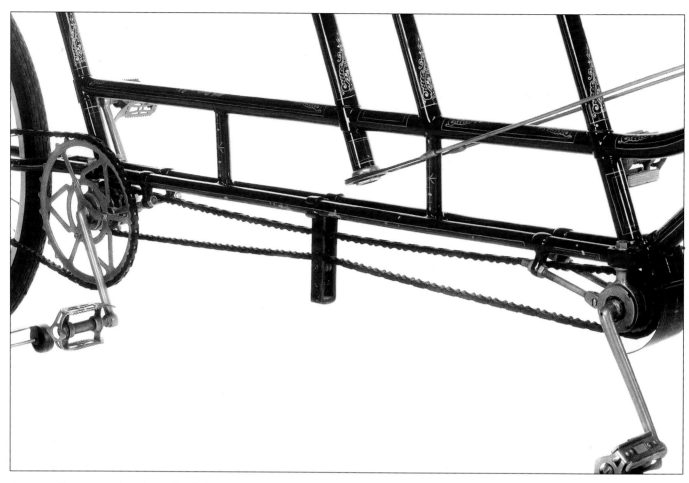

Due to the excessive length of the drive chain, a center-mounted tension device was used to maintain the proper level of slack.

units produced in a single year, the rate had fallen by over 75 percent. Many factors were to blame for this swift decline, but the appearance of the motor vehicle seems to have been the strongest. While the motorized vehicle was still a novelty to most, it sparked the imaginations of many who no doubt dreamed of purchasing one for themselves.

Improving roads, public transportation and a glut of cycle builders also added to the woes felt by most companies. The Arnold, Schwinn Company was not one of them, due to clever planning and a terrific product. The company did not record a single loss during the late 1890s' upheaval and collapse of the bicycle market. The total number of

bikes being built by Schwinn averaged about 26,000 units annually between 1895 and 1900.

By acquiring the defunct March-Davis Bicycle Company and its factory in 1899, Schwinn now had a new home for expanded production. One year later they built a brand-new facility for assembling their two-wheeled machines. Chicago would now be the permanent home for Arnold, Schwinn & Company. By 1903, more than 53,000 Schwinn bicycles were being built annually.

The fallout of the market caused several of the remaining firms to enter into a partnership, or trust. The American Bicycle Company was the spawn of this marriage. This trust seemed to pose a threat to

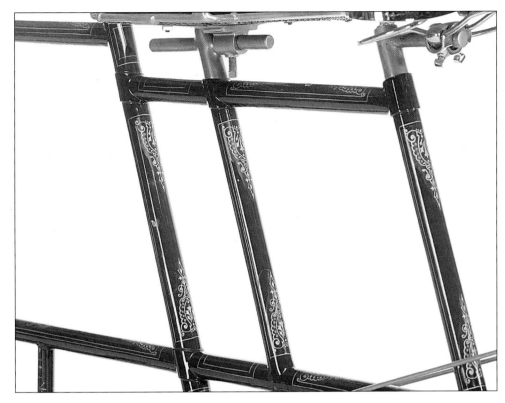

Nearly every segment of the tubular frame was festooned with ornate scrolls, pinstripes and trim.

the mighty Arnold, Schwinn & Company. Truth be told, the new conglomeration was a mess, with little or no real direction or leadership. Ignaz prided himself on beginning as, and remaining, a self-contained company, and he chided the efforts of the competition in his ads. The words "Our bicycles are NOT MADE by a TRUST" defiantly jumped off the printed page. By 1903, the American Bicycle Company had folded its tent after defaulting on its bond issue. Oddly enough, one of the men behind this boondoggle was none other than John D. Rockefeller, owner of Standard Oil and one of history's greatest industrialists.

Although the attempt to combine other companies failed, the "strength in numbers" train of thought remained strong for several decades after the collapse of the American Bicycle Company. Even the Schwinn company was experiencing huge losses in sales, with only 20,215 units being assembled in 1904. That number had fallen from over 53,000 units the previous year. Sales would rebound slightly in the next few years, finally returning to 54,000 in 1907. Unforeseen troubles in the bicycle market and inconsistent sales led Adolph Arnold to depart the firm in 1908. Ignaz bought out his partner's share, and the Schwinn family was now the sole owner of the firm. The Arnold, Schwinn & Company name would remain, however, until the end of the 1960s.

As soon as the bicycle craze hit the streets of America, bicycle racing became the rage. The results of the events were posted on the front pages of major newspapers as America now followed a new kind of hero. Schwinn bicycles were often the center of attention as the factory's teams claimed victory after victory.

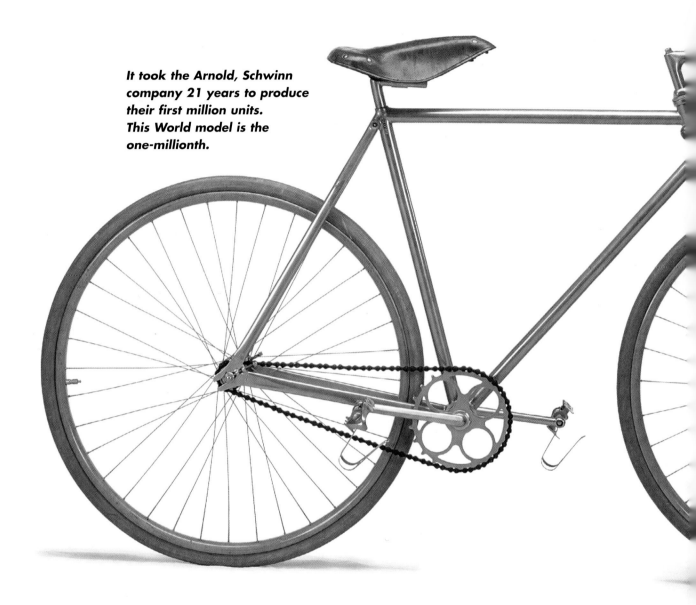

It took the Arnold, Schwinn company 21 years to produce their first million units. This World model is the one-millionth.

1896 saw the opening of a brand new cement racetrack in Chicago's Grant Park. This half-mile circuit was attended by a crowd of 25,000 fans at its initial event. Two of Schwinn's factory riders, Jimmy Michael and Johnny Johnson, set world records at the new venue on opening day.

The 1897 edition of Schwinn's World Catalog claimed that "more records had been broken on World" racing bicycles in one year than all other makes combined"—a proud statement that helped to push the Schwinn name to the top.

Bicycle racing encompassed a wide variety of events, and Schwinn proved their dominance in almost every class. From solo riders breaking half-mile, kilometer, and half-kilometer records to the popular paced racing, Schwinn products triumphed. Their racing machines carried riders in several configurations. Solo, tandem, triplet, quad and quint bicycles offered a dizzying array of racing variety. Fans were rabid in their quest to witness

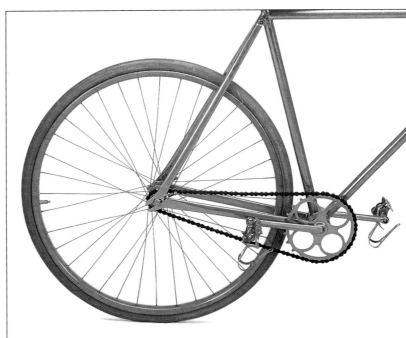

Built with no brakes, a single gear ratio and solid rubber tires, the World wasn't elaborate, but it sold as solidly as it was built.

Bicycle Museum of America

The World's earlier wooden grips were now replaced by units that featured a composite grip for comfort.

another distance or speed record fall to the Schwinn-mounted riders.

With the subsequent fall of the bicycle market, however, came a similar loss of appeal in racing. Headlines were no longer touting the results of an event, but focused on problems of the nation, although international events held some popularity until the advent of the second world war.

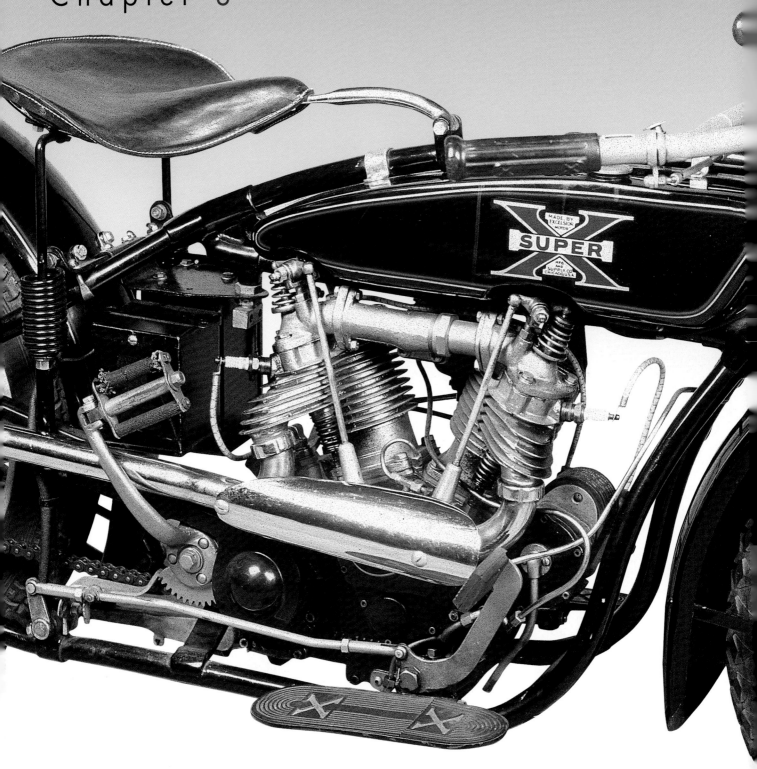

As the fever of bicycle racing was waning, Ignaz and his son Frank turned part of their attention to the expanding motorcycle market. With the introduction of the Indian name in 1902 and Harley-Davidson in 1903, the motorcycle industry was suddenly the place to be. Just as in the early days of the American bicycle, builders were popping up on every street corner with dreams of fame and fortune.

Wheels Through Time Museum

This well-worn journal was probably included in the materials that Ignaz reviewed before deciding to buy the Excelsior motorcycle brand.

The designers at Schwinn had been working on a motorcycle of their own creation, and had incorporated some futuristic components. While their work was impressive and ahead of its time, Ignaz saw a more efficient way of entering the fray.

Instead of building a new machine from the ground up, it made more sense to purchase an existing firm and use that as their way into the crowded field.

The year of 1910 found Ignaz and his son Frank W. on their way to a trade show in Atlantic City.

They were on a fact-finding mission to examine the state of current motorcycle offerings. A large group of manufacturers was present including Indian, Harley-Davidson and Excelsior. Since their introduction in 1905, the X models from Excelsior had proven to be quite popular but the company nevertheless was failing.

Ignaz decided to take a closer look at the company's books and decided soon after that it was a sound investment. With Excelsior's nearly $200,000 worth of orders pending, the acquisition appeared to be a win-win situation. Ignaz purchased the company for $500,000 in 1911 and was now in the motorcycle business for himself.

Using the same engineering prowess shown on their bicycles, the new and improved Excelsior machines proved to be well built and durable. No sooner had Ignaz purchased the company than the motorcycle industry went into high gear.

The resulting boon in sales added tremendously to the balance sheets of the firm. Not content to sell only single and twin-cylinder powered machines, the engineers at Schwinn started toying with the option of producing an inline, four-cylinder motor. This was not as easy as planned, but Ignaz's timing was once again perfect.

The Henderson Motorcycle Company of Detroit was on the edge of financial ruin and was seeking a buyer for their company. Henderson already built a four-cylinder machine, and Ignaz hoped to parlay existing technology into an even better version of the existing cycle. In 1917 Ignaz bought the ailing Henderson firm, extending his reach in the market. Once under his wing, the company was moved from Detroit to Chicago.

By enhancing the frame design of the existing four-cylinder models, Ignaz improved what was already one of the world's most graceful motorcycles. The revised four-cylinder models found new acceptance among riders and received new attention from law enforcement agencies across the country. The smooth running four-cylinder made a long day in the saddle livable. Excelsior and Henderson models were sold side by side, each offering a different style of riding and performance. A 1919 Excelsior was the first twin-cylinder motorcycle to break the 100 MPH mark.

The designers at Schwinn had been working on a motorcycle of their own creation, and had incorporated some futuristic components. Their work was impressive and ahead of its time.

Being the owner of Henderson, Excelsior, and Schwinn, Ignaz used all three marques on his lines of bicycle as well. Luring young bicycle riders into the den of motorcycle inequity by selling them like-named bikes was a good idea, but it failed to significantly improve sales.

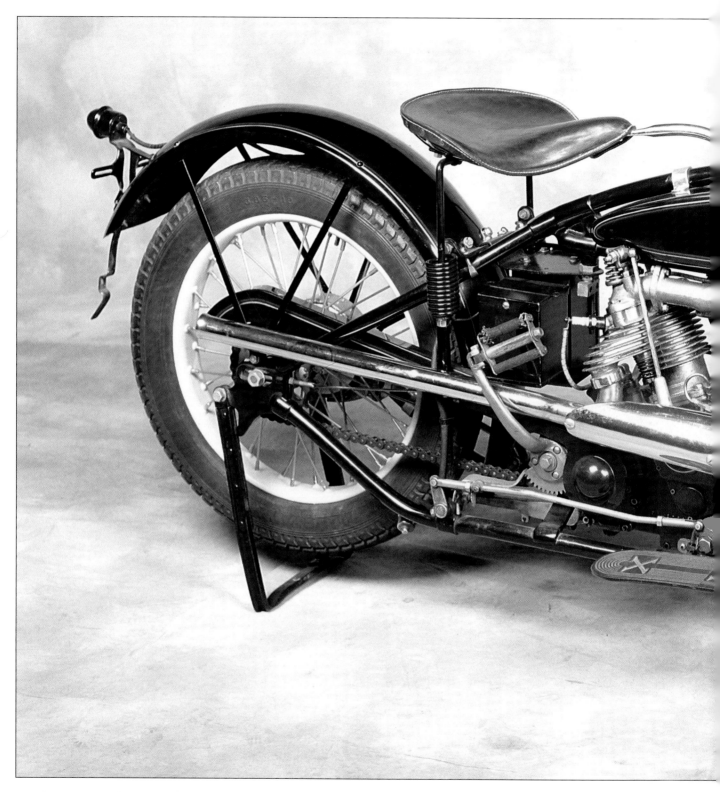

In 1925, a Super-X factory racer named Bob Perry was killed during an event. Tragedy seldom sold new machines of any sort, and the rider's death tainted Ignaz's view of the industry. Closely following this death came the Great Depression, further eroding sales of motorcycles. Adding insult to injury, Ignaz had taken a beating in the 1929 stock market crash and was growing weary of the workload he encountered each day.

Returning from a trip from Washington in 1931,

This 1925 Super X was powered by the proven twin-cylinder motor and was the most popular model in Schwinn's motorcycle lineup. Sadly, 1925 would be the year an Excelsior team rider would be killed during a race, thus putting a damper on Ignaz Schwinn's enthusiasm for motorcycles.

he gathered a small group of valued employees together. "Gentlemen, today we stop." With those four words, Excelsior and Henderson were no more. Ignaz retired soon after this announcement, allowing his son Frank W. Schwinn to take the reins of the company. It had been a good run for the motorcycle arm of the bicycle builder's empire, and changes in the bike market would soon bring many more variations to the world.

Schwinn

Despite Ignaz's retirement, the Arnold, Schwinn Company was far from shutting its doors. Ignaz son Frank W. was left in the wake, and was eager to take the reins of the company his father had spent so many years to create.

Frank W. possessed many of the same skills and traits of his father, and they would provide the basis for success. On top of those talents, Frank's mind was more amenable to travel and change. He saw the company for what it could be, not only what it had become.

Frank W. entered the engineering program at the Chicago Armour Institute after high school, but they were teaching him nothing in the ways of two-wheeled contrivances. His contact and involvement with the Arnold, Schwinn company proved to be the stronger draw, and he left college to focus his energies there.

Both father and son had an innate ability to think on the fly, and often created new designs with little or no notice. It was said that Ignaz would sketch new ideas in the dust of the shop floor with his cane, and Frank W., while using paper and pen, would do the same. Frank W. saw a much bigger picture for the existing company, and had plans to fulfill that destiny. He was displeased with the lack of growth at Schwinn and in the bicycle industry as a whole. He still saw great potential, and although a bit naive, he wanted bicycles to reach the same level of popularity they had in the 1890s. Of course powered vehicles now populated every road, and

One of the Schwinn built bikes sold under the Excelsior banner was the B-10-E Motorbike. The "fuel" tank was done in a style that mimicked those found on actual motorcycles, and the balloon tires delivered a smooth ride.

Bicycle Museum of America

people were accustomed to driving their cars or riding motorcycles by now. It would be a tall order to make the bicycle a highly desired purchase again.

There were several other mitigating factors that were dragging down the bicycle industry. Quality levels had fallen drastically as manufacturers attempted to create machines that could be sold cheaply but profitably. Large retail outlets such as Sears could sell an enormous quantity of units and offer affordable payment plans, things the independent shop owner could not. Quantity versus quality was becoming a losing battle for builders and sellers alike. Frank W. was determined to return to the days when quality was king, and he vowed to increase durability and performance while still turning a profit. It would be his savvy and unwavering vision that would make this a reality.

Despite his desire to do what seemed to be the impossible, Frank W. vowed to make the changes required. One variable not under his control was his inability to get suppliers to meet his demand for

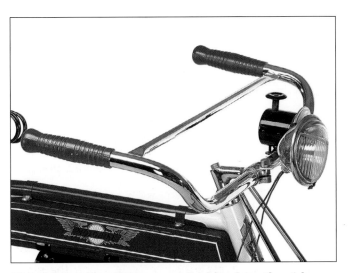

The chrome handlebars reached back to the rider, and were enhanced with the stout cross member for added strength, a Schwinn trademark.

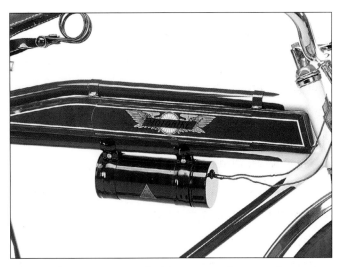

The tank was suspended between the two frame tubes, and the battery box hung below the lower tube, adding another touch of "motorcycle" to the bike.

high-quality components. There were only so many makers of chains and other needed bicycle parts, so they felt they had the power to control quality, or the lack thereof. Unable to produce every piece needed to build bicycles himself, Frank W. grew increasingly frustrated with the situation. It seemed that American buyers and builders cared little for quality as long as the machines were affordable. Frank W. saw this as a less than satisfying condition.

At the time, most bikes were built using inexpensive steel for the frames, and the welding and brazing were minimal at best. These factors, combined with the choke-hold of the component makers, cause Frank W. years of added frustration. It would appear that he was the only man who wanted to build a better bicycle and was willing to do whatever needed to meet that goal.

Being well traveled, Frank W. often scheduled trips to faraway lands to examine and experience other ways of life. The young Schwinn was also an avid reader who absorbed information like a sponge. He enjoyed traveling as long as the trip provided some insight to his life and business.

A trip to Germany in 1933 sparked a new level of inspiration in Frank W. He witnessed a much higher level of interest in bicycles while there, and people rode over terribly rough cobblestone streets with little complaint. The reason was the tires their bicycles were shod with. Unlike the thin, rubber units mounted to rims in the U.S., the German models had wide, air-filled donuts on the front and rear. These "balloon" tires made all the difference, and Frank W. returned home with a newfound passion. He saw the balloon tire as way to add

comfort, and therefore desirability, to the American-made bicycle.

With their dominance in the bicycle tire market, existing tire vendors scoffed at Frank's desire to make these newfangled tires and rims. Encountering an "if it ain't broke don't fix it" attitude, Frank W. realized he needed a new method of enticing them to see things his way. The U.S. Rubber Company, one of the largest in the country, had no time for his silly notions. Getting no help from them, Frank W. simply turned his attentions to other tire makers. Enjoying a long-term history with Firestone, who made rims for other vendors, Frank

1934 was the first year of production for the sleek Streamline Aerocycle, and while it was fairly popular, its sales were limited by its relatively high price price.

Bicycle Museum of America

W. requested that they reproduce the sample rims he'd brought back from Germany. Fisk Rubber agreed to produce the 5,000 tires Frank needed to complete his scheme. Troubles arose, however, when the Fisk tires didn't mate with the Firestone rims as they were designed to. Gathering all his bravado, Frank W. re-approached U.S Rubber and demanded they produce the tires he wanted. Threatened with losing business to an overseas producer and impressed with his moxie, the company agreed to make the tires he needed.

Obviously, just adding new tires to an existing bicycle was not what Frank W. had in mind. While

he battled with the tire and rim makers, he was busy engineering a heavy new frame to ride on the latest in tire design. By widening the frame and forks, and adding new strength to the entire layout, Frank W. was ready to peddle his latest creation to retailers.

Happy with what they already offered, they turned a blind eye to these new heavyweight machines. Claiming they would be too heavy and too expensive for most consumers, few embraced Schwinn's latest variation. With his usual level of determination turned up to 10, Frank W. continued to beat the bushes for a willing buyer. Just as things

Top: *The burgeoning aviation industry influenced the design of the Aerocycle, particularly its aerodynamic tank. Schwinn's claims for the new model included a welded frame that was "built like an aeroplane fuselage."*

Bottom: *The graphics, too, suggested the profile of a stoutly-designed aircraft.*

looked their darkest, Frank W. found an interested party: the Chicago Cycle Supply Company.

The Chicago Cycle Supply Company was one the country's biggest wholesale operations. They saw the value and quality of the latest Schwinn and agreed to carry the line. Their one major stipulation was that Schwinn could not sell the same models to the low-priced retailers. They wanted to have an exclusive product line that would be carried by the smaller, more service-oriented shops. After years of being forced to sell whatever they could get, these shops could offer the finest bicycles in the country, and even earn a profit doing so.

The B10-E Motorbike, introduced in 1933, was the first balloon tire model introduced, and it sold at a rapid pace. Although it cost the dealers a few dollars more per unit, they had trouble keeping them in stock. Turns out Frank W.'s idea to sell this type of bicycle wasn't so crazy after all. In less than a year, sales of balloon tire models would change the face of the bicycle industry, drawing competition from rival builders.

Suddenly everyone wanted to ride a balloon tire bike, and the industry responded with a wave of new offerings. Having been the first in the U.S. market, "Schwinn Built" bikes commanded and received the lion's share of the sales. While many of the larger retailers now carried balloon tire models, the Schwinns carried an added air of quality and long life. People were willing to spend a few extra dollars when they knew their new bicycle would last for many years to come. After years of browbeating just to get the attention of suppliers,

To complete the aviation theme, a battery-powered headlight was melded into the creation. The location and chrome bezel did nothing to detract from the aircraft motif.

Frank W. was now in charge.

A new twist in the retail world was large sellers wanting Schwinn bikes with their own store name applied to the frame. Schwinn responded to this need, and was soon selling bikes badged with over 100 different name plates. This allowed retailers to sell a high-quality, "exclusive" machine without requiring Schwinn to design special models. Even today, many Schwinn-built models can be found with names of famous and not-so-famous retailers on the steering head. A new method of selling bikes had been found, and Frank's company took full advantage of the situation.

With bicycle sales booming, Frank W. took the time to create some brand-new models. The balloon

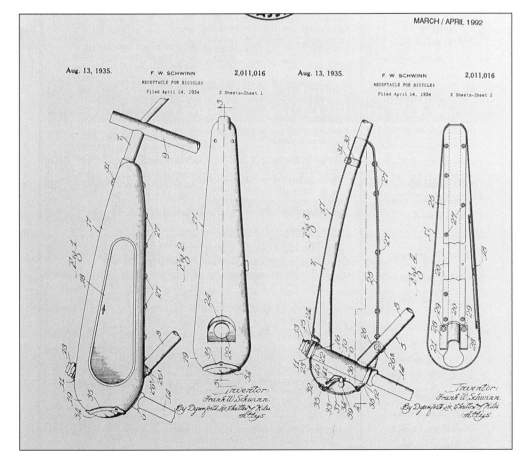

Dated August 13, 1935, this drawing illustrates the new horn tank design created by Schwinn and submitted for patent approval.

The Streamline continued the aviation theme and provided the rider with a softer ride through its front suspension.

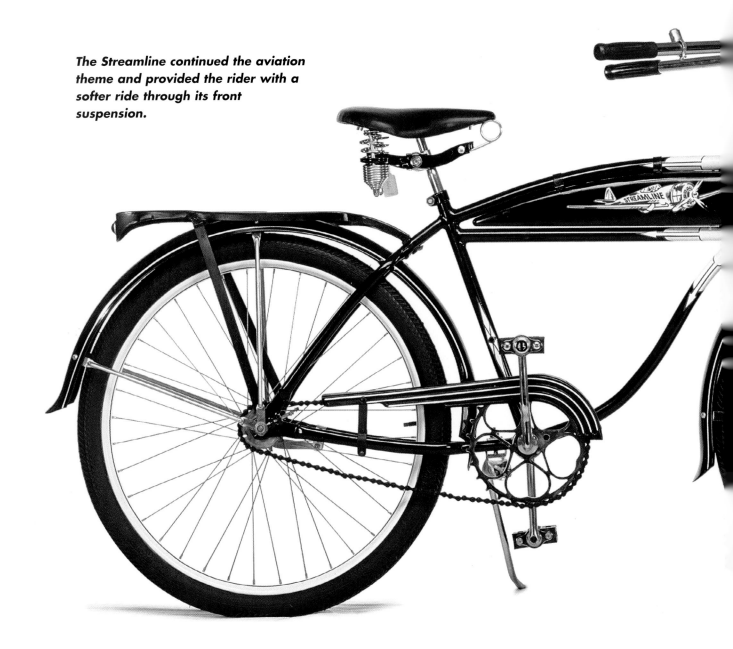

tire era coincided nicely with the expansion of the aviation industry, and his latest creations carried the theme to the streets. The 1934 Streamline Aerocycle, Model 34, was the first offspring of this bicycle/aviation marriage. Riding on comfortable balloon tires, the Aerocycle also wore the sleekest of design elements. With a frame-mounted tank that mimicked a plane's fuselage, the scene was set. Within the shapely walls of the tank was a space for tools, as well as a battery to power the head and tail

lights. Topping off the tank's lines were a flush-mounted headlight and aviator graphics. Original patent filings in 1934 described the new tank design as a "receptacle for bicycles"– hardly a flattering term. As time went by, "horn tank" became the more common designation.

The Aerocycle was a highly desired model, but the high cost of admission kept sales lower than hoped. Despite this, the Aerocycle did bring people into the Schwinn showrooms. Buyers may have

Bicycle Museum of America

Another aircraft-like tank was used on the Streamline, albeit without the built-in headlight.

wanted the high-priced Aerocycle but often left with another Schwinn that better met their financial constraints. Sales improved across the line, with units sold reaching an all time high of nearly 87,000 in 1934. This was a far cry from the dismal sales of bikes that barely reached 17,000 only two years earlier.

Sales continued to expand in 1935, and the total number of units sold reached just over 107,000. Part of this continued success was the introduction of

new models to meet with the needs of a wider variety of buyers. Walking into the showroom in 1935, an eager buyer would find a new model named the Motorbike alongside the Aerocycle. For some reason, the tank on the Motorbike was labeled as such, but the model was known as the Cycleplane. Even Schwinn promotional pieces had "Cycleplane" as the headline to sell the latest model. Borrowing several styling elements from the more expensive Aerocycle, the Motorbike/Cycleplane sold well. Still a solidly built piece, it was slightly dumbed-down to be more affordable. While not featuring all of the Aerocycle's expensive options, you could still find the electrical system powered by a battery stowed in the tank.

Sales for 1936 would prove to be Schwinn's best ever, with a total of over 201,000 units being sold. This figure was nearly double that of 1935, and it proved that Frank W. Schwinn had ideas that sold bicycles. Originally considered a rogue concept

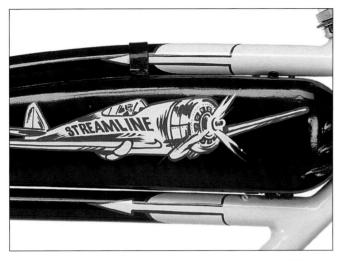

Top: *Reminiscent of the Corsair used by the military, the Streamline's graphics once again reminded riders how close they were to actually flying.*

Bottom: *The installation of the coil spring and support struts gave the front end of the Streamline a touch of suspension, adding to the overall comfort of the rider.*

man, he was now regarded as someone to be reckoned with.

Another new model rode onto the showroom floor for 1936. "The bicycle sensation of America" heralded the new (SA207) Autocycle. Equipped with a raft of unprecedented features, the Autocycle was an instant hit.

Breaking away from the aviation field a bit, the Autocycle joined the automobile fray instead. The curvaceous tank was trimmed with a pair of Stimsonite reflectors, coining the phrase "jeweled tank." These two reflectors were joined by a third mounted on the rear fender. Up front, a "fender bomb" adorned the top of the chrome fender, and a pair of bullet-shaped Seiss headlights lit the way. As was typical, the headlights were powered by a battery housed within the frame-mounted tank.

For the rider's comfort, a full floating saddle was added to the new model. A coil spring contained within the vertical frame tube compressed and rebounded to tame uneven street surfaces.

Probably the most stylish aspect of the Autocycle was the handlebar-mounted speedometer. The actual speedometer, a Stewart-Warner product, was suspended by a sleek crossbar that attached to both ends of the handlebar, near the grips. A pair of Bakelite buttons was used to honk the horn or illuminate the face of the speedometer.

The Autocycle remained near the top of the sales charts for many years. Enhancements on future models included a sprung front fork in 1938, as well as a cantilever frame and a chromed "feather" chain guard. A streamlined fender light was added in 1941, and an attached sidestand

The Autocycle was Schwinn's first foray into the car/bicycle design theme. This example is fitted with red rubber tires, a popular option of the day. This first-year model is devoid of the front spring, which was added in 1938.

joined the fray in 1946. The Autocycle was produced through 1949 but was not called by that name after 1946. It was merely known as the B6.

Sales of Schwinn-made bicycles tapered off a bit in 1937, reaching just under 169,000 for the year. Several important features were added for the year, and it was obvious that Frank was not resting on his laurels during the boom years.

Until 1937, stopping power on the majority of bicycles was handled by simple coaster brakes on one or both wheels. Frank W. Schwinn would once again set the bicycle world aflame with the introduction of his Fore-Wheel Brake. Modeled after the same units used on motorcycles and cars, this new addition make great strides in safety. Quality had always been a selling point for Schwinn bikes, but safety played a close second.

Along with increased sales came increased theft as bicycles grew in popularity. To thwart thieves, the New-Angle Cycelock was also introduced in

This austere prototype of the first Paramount sold in 1938 perhaps gave little suggestion that the model would become the most prestigious racing bike in the world.

1937. Touted as "The Final Solution of the Bicycle Theft Problem" in a 1935 trade publication, the new device helped keep bicycles in the hands of the rightful owners. Located in the lower end of the steering head, the Cycelock allowed you to lock the handlebars in one position, making it impossible to ride. A key unlocked the machine for use. Schwinn provided a one-year guarantee against loss when you purchased a bike with the new Cycelock.

The balloon tire race had been a long-running battle, and Schwinn had proven dominant in the marketplace. There were, however, riders who longed for a sportier machine that was lighter in weight and more purpose-built. A talented bike mechanic named Emil Wastyn was enlisted to assist in the design of just such a machine. Emil had a proven record in the race bike field, and was considered to be the best man for the job. Nineteen-thirty-eight would be the year the world was introduced to the Wastyn-designed Paramount line of racing bikes from Schwinn.

These machines were absolutely svelte when

The downward curve of the handlebars kept the rider in the optimum position for resistance to the wind.

Bicycle Museum of America

Built with the lightest alloys and finest materials kept the weight of the Paramount to just under 20 pounds.

"The Choice of Champions" was the claim made in this Schwinn comic book, and it was backed up by scores of racing victories.

compared to the rest of the Schwinn catalog. Weighing in at approximately 19 pounds, the Paramounts were stripped of all unnecessary gear. With ultra-lightweight frames made with chrome-moly tubing and only the finest mechanical components, the Paramounts were the finest machines ever built by Schwinn. Each Paramount was built to fit a rider's specific height and proportion, much like a tailor-made suit. They were not inexpensive, but competitive riders were willing to pay the price for a winning mount.

Over the next few years, the Paramount was making numerous new entries in the record books. One such record was the speed recorded by Alfred Letourneur. He rode a Paramount bicycle behind a modified midget race car to reach a top speed of 108.92 miles per hour. Due partially to corporate support from Schwinn, the Paramount bikes quickly became favorites of riders participating in 6-day events. The initial success of the Paramount,

The Autocycle was Schwinn's top of the line model and was packed with new and interesting features.

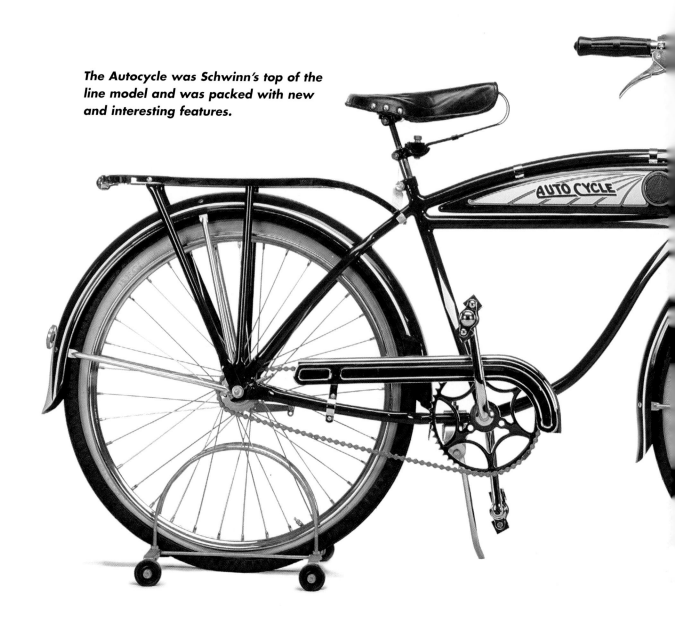

The "jeweled tank" was emblazoned with reflectors and trimmed with a set of louvers on its leading edge.

Dual headlights were encased in a pair of bullet-shaped housings to blaze the way through the night.

Bicycle Museum of America

as well as continued improvements to it, kept the name in the Schwinn catalogs until the early 1990s.

For buyers who wanted a lightweight machine but couldn't afford the entry fee of the Paramount, Schwinn devised a method of constructing a new series of machines. Built through a less costly assembly process, the Superior, Sports Tourer and Super Sport models would allow many new riders to join the high performance fray.

In contrast to the silver-soldered, chrome-moly, lugged frames of the Paramount line, the new Superior, Sports Tourer and Super Sport bikes employed chrome molybdenum (CrMo) straight gauge tubing, joined with brass fillet-brazed connections. Their assembly process required precise fitting of the frame tubes. Minor, unavoidable gaps between the tubes allowed brazing material to flow into the space and provide a secure joint. Steel sleeves were also brazed into the frame tubes at the points of contact for additional strength.

The Autocycle's front fender was adorned with a "bright metal, aerial bomb design, with high power reflective button," more commonly referred to as a fender bomb.

A speedometer was retained in a housing that stretched between the handgrips of the Autocycle. The speedometer was illuminated for use in the evening hours and was activated by pushing one of the buttons on the cross member.

The entire procedure delivered a frame that was lighter and stronger, yet less expensive than the ultra-premium Paramounts. While the new assembly did deliver on the weight saving front, little time was spent in cleaning up the fillet joints. While not sloppy, they did not have the same polished appearance as the Paramount frames.

There were other differences between the Paramounts and the Superiors. Paramount frames made their way onto a special finishing section for final paint and assembly. Superior frames, however, went into the standard production line for stamping, painting and all final assembly work. Superiors were painted in standard production colors, thus making them tough to pick out of a crowd. Whereas the Paramount line had its own series of serial numbers, the Superior models fell into the mix of all other Schwinns being built.

The Superior line of bikes was produced from 1938 to 1978, when the labor required to build them became outdated and unprofitable. The Varsity and Continental models satisfied the needs of most mid-level performance riders, and those who demanded high performance had a terrific array of available machines to choose from.

For those seeking glamour, the Hollywood was first produced for the 1938 model year. Although not badged as such, company advertising used the Hollywood moniker. The Hollywoods were well equipped with a sprung front fork, expander brakes, a graceful horn tank and whitewall tires. Pre-war models had safety lacing that helped keep garments from getting caught in the rear spokes.

The first run of the Hollywood lasted until 1948 when the Starlet was introduced. The Hollywood model would reappear in 1957 in a new middleweight configuration and remain in the lineup until 1982.

Another new model, the Cycle Truck, made its way into the lineup in 1939 but was more of a niche product than a widely accepted consumer item. The

Cycle Truck featured a full-size frame with balloon tires at both ends. The rear wheel was of typical dimensions but the front wheel was much smaller to allow for the installation of a large carrying compartment. The frame was engineered so that the weight of the compartment and its contents was carried by the frame, not by the front wheel. Designed for use as a simple delivery vehicle, many small operations took advantage of this practical machine.

Always seeking ways to improve sales, in 1939 Schwinn introduced the Lifetime Guarantee on their entire lineup of bicycles. Covering the frame and most major components, Frank W. Schwinn did not consider this action to be risky. Another radical choice he made was to avoid the usual outlets for his product. Bicycles could be purchased at a variety of retailers, but none offered the level of customer service he wanted. Catering more heavily to the smaller, independent shops, Frank W. saw a better way of servicing buyers.

In the latter part of the 1930s, one of Schwinn's largest wholesalers in California was in dire financial straights. Frank dealt with the dilemma by stepping in and taking the helm of the operation. With almost 160 dealers being serviced by the wholesaler, the potential loss of sales was huge, and that was the last thing Frank W. had in mind. Once control was regained, Schwinn began shipping bikes directly to the retail shops, not through the sickly wholesaler. While risky—Frank W. had thin hopes of being paid for the shipped bicycles— this new business model satisfied the needs of the shops selling the bikes and created a new way of doing business.

Coined the "dealer-direct" system, the new structure allowed the Arnold, Schwinn Company to lower their costs through the classic strategy of eliminating the middleman, thus creating a better profit margin for the retailers. Yet another offshoot of this new way of selling bicycles was the high level of contact between the manufacturer and retailer. This newfound relationship would benefit both Schwinn and his dealers for many years to come.

Another popular option was grip-end reflectors.

The pogo seat provided another measure of comfort to the rider. A coil spring held in the seat post provided the springiness needed to cushion the ride.

The DX model was built for those who lacked the funds for a more exotic Schwinn model.

A lower-priced version of Schwinn's other bikes, the DX nevertheless came complete with splashy tank graphics.

The Schwinn family had always believed in the high quality of their product, and knew from experience that if a part were going to fail, it would happen within the first year. Most of the industry stuck to their one year-guarantees, giving Schwinn offerings another leg up on the competition. Frank W. was often heard to say that he would "rather have 99 of 100 customers take advantage of me than have one customer not treated right."

The year 1940 would see some improvements and features added to the existing lineup of Schwinn bikes and a new lower-priced entry to the catalog. The New World model was added in 1940, and sold for a mere $32. When compared to the pricey Paramount at $75 and the medium performance Superior at $50, the New World offered the buyer a lot of value for the money. Despite its lower selling price, the New World shared many features of the Superior line. Lightweight 1-1/4-inch wheel rims, machined steel hubs and three-piece crank sets provided durability. In less than a year, the Sturmey-Archer three-speed

hub was added to the component list. Not yet widely accepted in the U.S., the three-speed was a common sight overseas.

The Autocycle family would grow by one model with the introduction of the Autocycle Super Deluxe. Combining all the features of the Autocycle and Autocycle Deluxe, the Super went one step beyond. With expander brakes at both wheels and whitewall tires (commonly called "black and whites") added to the already lengthy list of features on the standard and Deluxe models, there was little left to the imagination.

As always, Schwinn tried to satisfy all the market's demands, and to meet the needs of the lower priced models, the D Series were as bare bones as the Autocycle Super Deluxe was decked out. But even the lowly D model could be purchased in a myriad of colors, and some of the ensembles came with color coordinated painted rims. Attempting to fulfill the needs of every conceivable requirement of the bicycle's use, a selection of wheel hubs was also available to meet demand. Everything from a Schwinn-Built Standard Front Hub to the more exotic Large Flange Heavy-Duty Fore-Wheel Hub could be purchased to customize your bike to satisfy your dreams.

With America bracing for World War II, there were no new models or improvements made between 1941 and 1945. There didn't have to be. Concerned over the possibility of having their automobile tires and gasoline rationed, consumers flocked to Schwinn dealers to buy virtually any dependable machine that required no fuel.

In an attempt to keep up with growing demand during these times, Schwinn production hit an all-time high of nearly 225,000 units in 1940 and just under 347,000 in 1941. The earlier acceptance of the products sold by the Arnold, Schwinn & Company proved to be invaluable on the wartime homefront.

Lean supplies of all wartime materials caused drastic reductions in Schwinn's bicycle output over the next 3 years. A government contract for 10,000 military bikes per year kept a few of the factory lights on, but the production lines were generally quiet. Many of the machines used to produce bicycles were pressed into military duty. Untold thousands of rounds of artillery ammunition were produced using the same machines that had previously cranked out bike components. The versatility of the Schwinn company proved once again to be invaluable.

A strong feeling of camaraderie developed during the war years. People working at Schwinn were drawn into a tightly-knit group that resembled a large family. Work ethic had always been strong at Schwinn, but the war efforts only enhanced it. In 1944 the company was bestowed

with the government's Army-Navy E-Award, an honor reserved for defense contractors who kept up with wartime needs. The E flag was flown with pride at the plant in Chicago as Schwinn joined an honored group of 233 companies who earned the right to fly it in the Windy City.

The previously introduced Cycle-Truck became a popular item when pressed into military service delivering mail at Naval bases. Most of the bicycles built during this period were finished in the standard olive drab to meet with government specifications. With an end to the war in sight, and materials becoming more available, 1945 output reached almost 99,000 units, and better days were on the horizon.

Fitted with the "sweetheart sprocket," called such due to its heart-shaped openings, the drive chain was also protected by the painted chain guard complete with the Schwinn logo.

The Cycle Truck was first introduced in 1939 and quickly became a favorite of deliverymen across the country. The example seen here is the S1, which included the small front basket.

The small basket model (S1) still held a large quantity of goods, but the large basket version (S2) featured a wraparound contrivance that engulfed the front end of the bike and handlebars.

The flat panel mounted between the frame tubes was a perfect location for company propaganda.

Schwinn

The Postwar Boom

Chapter 5

With the war now behind them, Schwinn, along with the rest of the country, was ready to get back into the fun of living. Returning GI's had money to spend and the general public had plenty of pent-up buying demand. Things never looked better for the Schwinn factory.

Whizzers first appeared during World War II as a way to stretch fuel and rubber inventory. This 1948 model is an LS-10.

Although no new models or improvements had been implemented since 1940, the Schwinn R&D department had not been asleep. The year of 1946 saw the introduction of a bevy of new features that made the Schwinn collection more appealing than ever.

A fold-up kickstand was now an integral part of the frame design, saving riders the trouble of finding a convenient wall to lean their Schwinns on. Mounting lugs for the chain guards were now part of the frame, and rear fenders were now attached using separate mounting points.

Larry Anderson

Post-war production was off to a rousing start with over 302,000 Schwinns built in 1946. The following year saw another leap in assembled units with a total of nearly 487,000.

Alongside the pedal-powered bicycles, Frank W. Schwinn renewed his interest in the motorized bicycle called the Whizzer. Although the Whizzer was built by another firm, Schwinn's heavy-duty frames were most often used to support the Whizzer's single-cylinder motor. With a top speed nearing 40 miles per hour, the Whizzer needed the best frame money could buy. Along with its zippy

The tiny motors fit perfectly within the well-built Schwinn frames, and this strength allowed the Whizzers to reach a top speed of almost 40 miles per hour.

This housing protected the drive pulley from the rider's pant leg. The power was delivered via belt to the rear wheel.

top speed, a Whizzer could return up to 125 miles per gallon, making it a thrifty way to get around in the post-war world. Before the end of 1948, more than 200,000 Whizzers were being sold annually. The majority of these units were built on Schwinn frames.

However, seeing a benefit in building their own frames instead of buying them from Schwinn, Whizzer "borrowed" the design of the patented cantilever frame and began producing their own. No sooner did Schwinn get the word of this change than legal action was threatened. After some rattling of swords, Whizzer vice president Bill Burch met with Frank W. Schwinn at a conference. Once the two had exchanged heated words and veiled threats, they decided to convene for lunch. The two idea men were able to combine their thoughts into less destructive actions, and things turned positive quickly. Over a simple meal they reached an accord. Not only were thorny legal issues put aside, but Ray Burch was later hired by Frank W. to head up a new and aggressive advertising campaign for Schwinn.

A new model for the ladies was also introduced in 1948, replacing the Hollywood: the Starlet. Listed as a heavyweight, the new Starlet was offered to the feminine public in an array of pastel finishes including Windswept Green, Luscious Lavender, Summer Cloud White and Holiday Rose.

In addition to the palette of colors, the Starlet was also trimmed heavily with a horn tank, rear carrying rack, chrome wheels and headlight. A Schwinn script logo was placed on the horn tank, and a Starlet logo was found on the chain guard. For those ladies seeking even more, a sprung front fork and whitewall tires could be added to the order sheet. Nineteen fifty-six would be the final year for the heavyweight Starlet, but a new middleweight variant was sold starting in 1957.

Nineteen forty-eight would mark the passing of Ignaz Schwinn. His 88 years had produced some of the world's greatest bicycles, a trend that would go on long after his demise. The Arnold, Schwinn Company produced more than 600,000 units in 1948, with many equally strong years to come. Ignaz had built more than a great bicycle. He had created an empire.

Delivering almost 125 miles per gallon, Whizzers didn't need a huge fuel tank to meet the needs of most riders.

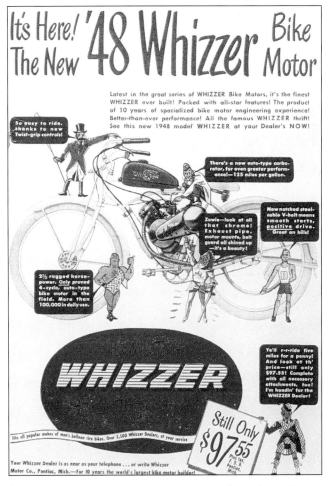

The 1948 Whizzer motor was touted as the wise way to go and was touted as "great on hills!"

Schwinn

The Black Phantom Era

Chapter 6

Schwinn's 1949 models would introduce the world to one of the company's most popular designs ever to roll out of the factory doors.

The Phantom models were released in 1949–not all of them the famous Black variety. This 1950 Red Phantom proves the point.

Bicycle Museum of America

Top left: *Among the many eye-catching features of the Phantoms were its curvaceous tanks complete with chrome horn buttons. The Cycelock was another Schwinn innovation seen on the Phantoms.*

Top right: *The 1950 Phantom was the first to have its name painted on the chain guard.*

Bottom left: *The chromed front fenders were fitted with a companion Fenderlite, first seen on 1940 models.*

For smaller riders who still desired a Phantom,
24″ tire versions (J29) were sold to meet the need.

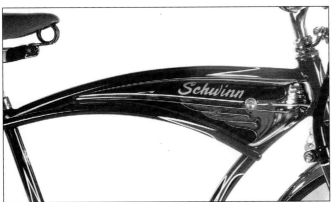

With the exception of tire size, the smaller
Phantoms were identical to the 26″ models in
every way, including the painted and chromed
horn tank.

The beautifully decorated chain guard was also
used on the smaller Phantoms.

The Black Phantom was not built around a cutting-edge frame design, but it embodied a new level of style that would become an instant classic. With the patented cantilever frame beneath, the Phantoms glittered with more chrome than ever seen before on a bicycle. A decade later Detroit would also apply enormous amounts of polished metal to their cars. Perhaps the Phantoms were trendsetters outside of their realm, too?

Almost every conceivable feature was used on the Phantom line. A chromed and painted tank, complete with a built-in horn button, a chromed front suspension and the sleek Fenderlite were only a few of the highlights. In contrast, the chain guards

Even the smaller Phantoms were prone to theft, but the Cycelock was on duty to keep your Phantom in your possession.

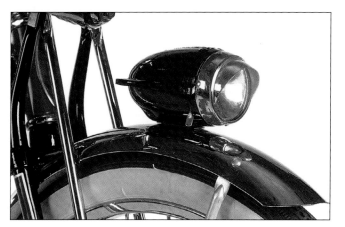

While the full-size Phantoms featured a sleek Fenderlite, the 24" model came with a Delta Rocket Ray headlight attached to the front fender.

In addition to the Phantom name, the chain guards were trimmed with a scalloped design to further enhance the theme.

were merely painted for the 1949 models, but subsequent models would feature "Black Phantom" graphics and the "Schwinn Approved" badge. In the 1949 models, Phantoms were also sold only with 26-inch frames while from 1950 through 1954 they could be had with an optional 24-inch frame. The smaller models were fitted with a Schwinn Delta Rocket Ray headlight in place of the Fenderlite found on the 26-inch models. Starting at $59.95, the Phantom was not within reach of every rider.

Unlike Ford's Model T, the Phantom was offered in colors other than black. There were red and green Phantoms sold, but the Black Phantom was by far the most coveted. A girl's Phantom was sold in 1955, and it was given a blue color scheme. For some reason, the ladies' version of the Phantom was only sold for four months and then disappeared from the roster.

All the features of the Phantom added up to a bike that weighed nearly 70 pounds. It did provide

Both front and rear tires on this example are adorned with stylish mud flaps, again with reflectors for greater visibility.

The wheel hubs had circular chrome trim pieces that included built-in reflectors as seen here.

a comfortable ride, but was by no means a lightweight bike. Fully chromed tubular rims and spokes were shod with whitewall tires, adding more appeal to the Phantom line.

The built-in Cyclelock and automatic stoplight were found as safety features. Braking on the entire family of Phantoms was provided by single-speed coaster brakes in the rear hub.

The Phantoms were sold until 1959, when the riding public began asking for a lighter machine. Proof of the timeless design of the Phantom was made evident when a replica Phantom was sold in 1995. With Schwinn now being owned by the Scott Sports Group, the reintroduced Phantom sold extremely well. Although not as desirable as an original model, the public was still happy to ride their new Phantoms home in great numbers.

While the Phantom was the big news for 1949, it wasn't the only new machine to hit the dealers' floors. For those whose finances would not permit the luxurious Phantom to be ridden home, the

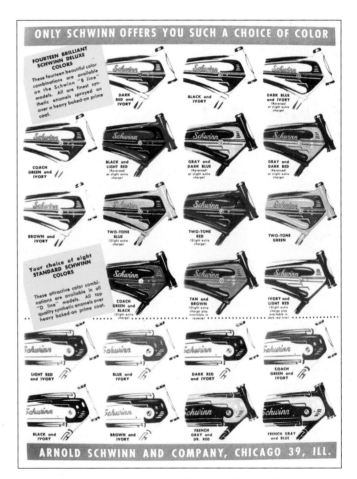

One of Schwinn's strong suits was their ability to offer the buyer a wide variety of options. This sales sheet shows the myriad of color choices available.

The ladies' Phantom appeared in 1955 but was built only for a four-month period between January and April.

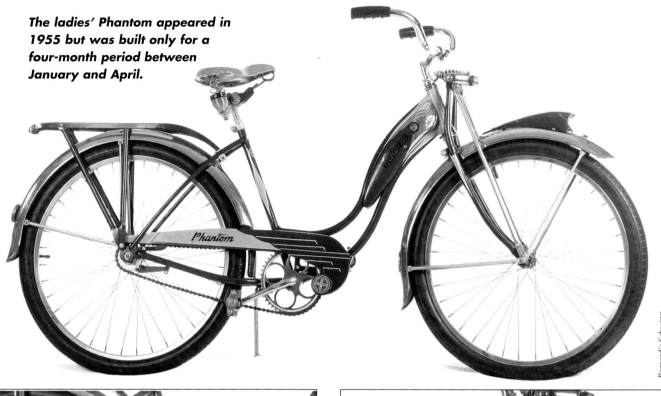

Barnard's Schwinn

The chain guard called out the Phantom name and was finished in a two-tone color scheme unlike the monotone versions found on the men's models.

The sleekly sculpted horn tank was still used on the ladies' model but had far less chrome trim than its men's-version counterpart.

Panther Model D-27 appeared in 1950 and was a great alternative. Fairly well equipped, the Panther was built using the older Motorbike style frame versus the newer cantilever design. It still featured a chromed sprung fork, chrome-trimmed tank and fenders, along with chrome rims and Delta Rocket Ray headlight. Whitewall tires were also included on the lower priced Panthers. Delivered in one of three different two-tone color combinations, the Panther still provided plenty of style. Two-tone green, two-tone red, or the black and red version could be had. The girls Panther Model D-77 was available only in two-tone blue.

Alongside the Panther in 1951 was the girls-only Starlet Model D67. Finished in either Holiday Rose and Summer Cloud White, or Windswept Green

The Panther cost a few dollars less than the Phantom but offered a similar array of features.

Bicycle Museum of America

The Fenderlite was also used on both the men's and ladie's version of the Phantom.

Two-tone green paint was one of many options available. Once again the name appeared on the chain guard.

and Luscious Lavender, they came fitted with white rubber grips and a Koroseal-top saddle. The same saddles were used on the Panthers but were finished in tan. The first edition of the Panther would remain in the Schwinn lineup through 1954 as a heavyweight bike and would return in 1959 after a significant weight loss.

The purebred racing Paramounts (Model P32) continued in the Schwinn lineup, but sales never reached any significant numbers. Those seeking a bicycle built solely for the purpose of racing were not the dominant market they once were. The Paramount Sport Touring model (P31 for the men, P81 for the ladies) offered a more street-friendly riding position and more chrome trim, but still carried a high price tag even when compared to

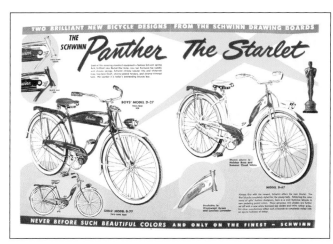

The Panther was marketed alongside the Starlet. Both were described as "brilliant new designs."

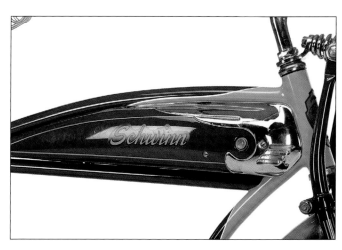

The tank was the highlight of the Panther's styling, complemented by an eye-catching combination of chrome and polished paint.

This 1951 ad shows a Phantom finished in red and highlights the long list of Schwinn's quality features.

The front forks were sprung, helping absorb the bumps thrown in the Panther's path.

The Panther's front fender was also ornamented with the official Schwinn Delta Rocket Ray headlight.

Perhaps the one bike from Schwinn that we all remember, the Black Phantom was first seen in 1949 and went on to become a timeless classic.

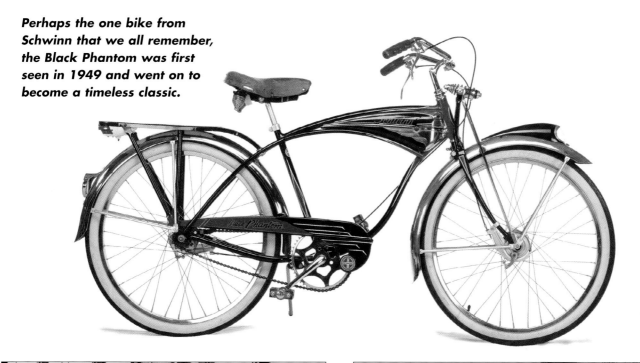

As if you didn't know, the chain guard told you this was THE Black Phantom.

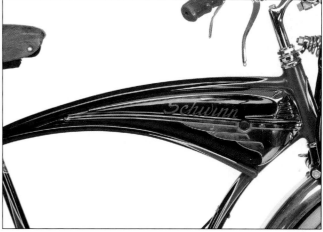

The swooping fuel tank, clad in black and chrome, was the pinnacle of bicycle design at the time.

other Schwinn offerings.

An additional heavyweight model, the Hornet, was introduced in the early 1950s. These bikes, while still stylish, were simpler in design and were not as well equipped as the Phantoms and Panthers. The Hornet was first released for 1951 sales and was delivered with a painted frame, wheels and horn tank. A simple headlight kept the Hornet at the lower end of the Schwinn catalog. Sold in a variety

of styles including those to fit boys, girls and juveniles, it filled a niche in the market. The Hornet would remain as a heavyweight until 1955, being replaced by a middleweight model in 1956.

By this time Schwinn's onetime antagonist Ray Burch had been hired away from Whizzer to revitalize Schwinn's marketing and advertising campaigns. It was 1950 when Burch first got a look at the existing dealer network assembled by

Although first used in 1940, the Fenderlite looks right at home atop the chromed fender of the Black Phantom.

Mounted beneath the rear luggage rack was another safety feature: a working taillight.

Complete with a banking aircraft in the background, ads for the Phantoms captured the hearts and pocketbooks of both young and old.

Schwinn. He found an unexpectedly high number of 15,000 "dealers" spread across the country. Under closer scrutiny, it was discovered that many of these retailers were not actually bike shops, but non-related operations that sold an occasional unit or two for Schwinn. This loose arrangement had to be changed in order to further grow the company.

Unannounced visits to some of these ragtag outlets showed Burch and Frank W. just how bad things had become. Poorly displayed models that were several years out of date and baskets of "defective" parts that only needed minor adjustments to fix were just a few examples of what they found.

Even with this appalling discovery, Schwinn and Burch were not hasty in eliminating those retailers selling the Schwinn bikes in less than desirable conditions. What was needed was a way to focus their attention of the retailers who did the best job of marketing and selling the Schwinn catalog of bikes. Although the numbers were rough, it appeared that a vast majority of the units was being sold by a tiny percentage of the dealers. These bike-savvy retailers knew how to cater to the customers' needs and sell them more than just a bicycle.

Larry Andersen

The Whizzer Peacemaker ran with an enlarged 199cc motor and included a wide variety of comfort and convenience items.

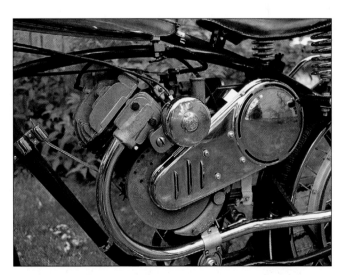

Power to the rear wheel was again provided by the pulleys hidden beneath this chrome cover.

A pair of basic coil springs provided the rider with a modicum of comfort on the open road.

The Deluxe model speedometer was a bit optimistic with a top speed posted at 80 miles per hour, but it also functioned as an odometer.

Impromptu dealer visits continued as ways were sought to pare down the long list of people selling Schwinn merchandise. Frank V. Schwinn, Frank W.'s son, would often ride along with Ray Burch as he visited these retail operations. It often seemed that it didn't take much to sell a Schwinn bicycle, despite their sometimes higher sticker price. When the showroom was clean, well-lit and stocked with gleaming bikes, what parent could say no?

Of course it wasn't really that easy, but a well-run showroom made it look that way. By the time the culling of sellers was complete, only about 2,000 retailers were left with Schwinn bikes to sell. These remaining outlets would be known as total-concept stores. The additional moniker of "Schwinn authorized dealer" lent an air of achievement and drew people to the new and improved outlets.

Rolled out in 1951, the Hornet was one of many choices for the Schwinn buyer.

Bicycle Museum of America

The Phantom was advertised alongside the lower-priced Wasp, just to show the world the breadth of Schwinn's offerings.

The Hornet moniker and logo were found on the painted chain guard. The Hornet's wheel rims were also painted rather than chromed, keeping the cost down.

Even being offered in the less expensive category, the Hornet came fully equipped with a Schwinn tank.

The Hornet was even delivered with a headlight mounted to the front fender.

Despite the fact that Schwinn now had fewer retail locations, sales continued to thrive.

On the cusp of the new middleweight's introduction, the Wasp was introduced in 1954. Still riding on balloon tires, it would replace the Phantom on the latter's demise in 1959 and continue on until 1965. Sold in basic trim, the Wasp was available in boys', girls' and juvenile styles.

The bulk of Schwinn's reputation and success had been based on the heavyweight machines they had created virtually singlehandedly. A European influence that helped spark the balloon tire era, but Schwinn had done much to improve the breed. As durable and comfortable as the heavy balloon tire bikes were, people were being exposed to the new medium weight bikes being brought in from overseas. Not only were these bikes lighter but they offered more panache for the same or less money than Schwinn's competing models. Obviously something had to change.

Available in 1955, the first Corvettes from Schwinn were single or three-speed models.

The front luggage rack was "Schwinn Approved"-imported from the Mayweg Company in Germany.

Therefore in 1952 Schwinn introduced a line of new middleweight bikes. Although the "middleweight" designation suggested an entirely new way to build a lightweight machine, there were few differences between them and the heavyweight versions.

The biggest change was the application of narrower rims. The balloon tires rode on 2-1/8-inch wide S-2 rims, while the first middleweights rolled on 1-3/4-inch S-7 hoops. Higher air pressures of between 45 and 50 psi made the bikes feel more responsive than those with the lower-rated balloon tires. This lower rolling resistance combined with lighter components created a bike that weighed "only" 50 pounds or so. This new figure was hardly considered svelte, but when compared to a fully loaded Phantom, the benefit was obvious. Basic frame design still hinged on the patented cantilever model, but subtle changes were used on the Typhoon in 1962.

Hoping to connect to the already popular vehicle from Chevrolet, the name Corvette suggested speed and sportscar-like agility.

Another page from a Schwinn comic/sales book touts the Corvette as "the World's Most-Copied Bicycle."

The Traveler provided the rider with plenty of comfort and convenience in a lightweight package. The generator-driven headlight allowed for nighttime riding as well. The example seen here is a three-speed.

The Traveler was equipped with a spring-loaded front carrier rack for storage.

Much of the American automotive world was being by passion for the all-new Corvette first introduced in 1953. To capitalize on this fervor, Schwinn named their first middleweight the Corvette.

The first Corvette bicycles were rolled out for the 1955 model year, and they would be included in the catalog until 1965. The last examples of the Corvette were labeled Corvette II. Both men's and ladies' versions were sold, but the ladies' models would be replaced by fresher tin in 1959.

Two different Corvette models were available the first year, both Deluxe in designation. You could have your Corvette with either a three-speed or single-speed coaster hub. Whitewall tires were standard, as well as the front-mounted carrier rack. Actually produced by the Mayweg Company in Germany, the rack was still a "Schwinn Approved" item and added a new level of versatility to the bike.

Braking on the three-speed models was provided by a pair of hand-operated caliper brakes. The rear unit required an additional mounting bracket, and the front end utilized a different fork casting to accommodate the brake assembly. The cable-operated gear selector was mounted on the right half of the handlebars. This cable mechanism screamed of European technology and added undeniable appeal.

The bulk of the Corvettes built rolled on 26-inch frames, but you could also buy a smaller 24-inch version if the rider's physique required such. As always, the Corvette was sold in a myriad of colors. In 1955, Corvettes could be purchased in your choice of white, black, Radiant Red, Radiant Blue or Radiant Green. Future options would include Coppertone, as well as the later "Flamboyant" hues.

During production of the Corvette, a new option was made available to the rider. The addition of the Bendix Automatic rear coaster brake hub provided two speeds, and a small amount of back-pedal movement was all it took to switch from one speed to the other. First used by Schwinn in 1960, it can be spotted by the three painted stripes of yellow or red on its outer housing.

An obscure variation of the Corvette was sold for two years starting in 1961. The five-speed variant may have been created to keep the pace with the imported competition, but wasn't enough

Although a subtle graphics application was selected, the Traveler name was still applied to the chain guard.

to keep the option around. The introduction of the ten-speed Continental and Varsity models made quick work of the five-speed Corvette.

Another new Schwinn for 1954 bearing an automotive name was the Jaguar. The first models were of the heavyweight/balloon tire variety, but they were removed from the catalog after 1955. The 1954 and 1955 models were outfitted with some rare options. In addition to the whitewall balloon tires, the Jaguars featured three-speed hubs and hand operated brakes at both wheels. A long list of accessories was also present, making the Jaguar a desirable choice for those who opted against buying a Phantom.

The Jaguars returned as middleweight models for 1957 and 1958, and were now labeled Mark IIs. The entire pride of Jaguars was well equipped, with Phantom-like tanks, chromed fenders and plenty of accessories. There were no ladies models made. Also, Jaguars were never built in any other frame size except for the 26-inch. From 1959 to 1962, the Jaguar became the Mark IV, but no Mark IIIs were produced. Mark IVs featured chrome and painted chain guards, as well as a second carrier rack on the rear wheel.

The Mark V Jaguar appeared for 1963 with the latest in sleek horn tank and a sprung front fork. Until the introduction of the Mark VI in 1965, the

Jaguars could be purchased with one, two or three-speed hubs. The Mark VI was sold only with single or two-speed hubs and coaster brakes.

Other entries in the 1955 catalog were the American and the Tiger.

Another new Schwinn for 1954 bearing an automotive name was the Jaguar. The first models were of the heavyweight/balloon tire variety, but they were removed from the catalog after 1955. The 1954 and 1955 models were outfitted with some rare options.

The American models were pitched to the riding public as 100% American-made in an effort to stanch sales of the European influx. Sold in 24-inch and 26-inch versions of boys' and girls' frames, the appeal and sales were terrific. An optional 20-inch coaster brake model as also seen on order sheets for 1955 but would disappear by 1956.

Production of American models ran through 1958 before slipping off the radar screen. In 1961 the American line was reintroduced. This second wind would last until 1966 when all production of Americans ceased. The 1961s could be purchased in a 20-inch, 24-inch or 26-inch variety. Only the 24-inch and 26-inch 1961 models would be fitted with a two-speed, Bendix Automatic hub. The 20-inch would roll with a single-speed coaster brake arrangement. To cater to an even more segmented market, the American would appear in several additional configurations for 1962.

The Deluxe American added whitewall tires, slim line horn tank, headlight and chrome carrier to the existing American model. The King Size American was sold in 1962, 1963 and 1964 and was designed for taller adults and teens. The frame dimensions were increased at several points including the seat down tube and head tube.

The Heavy Duty American featured heavier gauge spokes made from 120-gauge steel matched to a heavy-duty front hub and larger saddle. This model was also sold in 1962, 1963 and 1964.

Nineteen sixty-five found the Deluxe, King Size, and Heavy Duty Americans gone from the roster. To make matters more interesting, a sprung fork model was added to the standard American listing. This variant was simply noted as an "American w/Spring-fork" in the dealer listings. Color choices for the American models included blue, red, green, black and gold. A red, white and blue crest was added to the chain guard and frame seat tube.

Yet another entrant to the 1955 lineup was the Tiger. Built around the Schwinn cantilever frame, the Tigers all wore a band of checkered graphics on their seat-tube. Equipment on the standard Tigers was basic and included a three-speed hub and

The Cadet's speedometer was built by Stewart-Warner and helped the rider keep track of speed and miles logged.

A brightly-jeweled reflector adorned the rear fender for added safety.

caliper brakes. For the model years 1955 and 1956 there were both boys' and girls' varieties, with either 24-inch or 26-inch frames.

For 1957 the smaller option was dropped, and for 1959 the bike was marketed for boys only. To expand the potential customer base, the Tiger was sold with a choice of one, two or three-speed hubs in 1959. The 24-inch model was reintroduced for 1959 as well. This in-and-out routine was repeated in 1962 when the smaller, juvenile frame model was again eliminated from the catalogs. The Tiger bikes were built until 1964 when the model was

dropped completely.

Another fresh face for Schwinn was the Racer, first sold late in 1955. In an effort to maintain a competitive edge with the imported models, the Racer was well equipped. Three-speeds, hand brakes and a price of only $49.95 made the new model a popular choice for first-time buyers of lightweight bikes. According to advertising of the time, Schwinn offered more than 65 models in many different price categories.

The Starlet, last seen in 1948 as a balloon-tire heavyweight, was back in 1957 as a middleweight

The Jaguar Mk II appeared in 1957, but the Mk IV as seen here was released in 1959 and sold through 1962.

The chain guards on late-model Jaguars were finished in painted chrome while the Mk IIs were painted.

model. The name would change to Starlet II in 1965 and to Starlet III for its final run until 1970. A variety of frame sizes were available during the entire production run, and 20-inch, 24-inch and 26-inch were the players. No real consistency was apparent during the Starlet's 13-year stint as a middleweight. The rear hub could be had in the usual range of single, double or triple speed variations.

The Starlets came equipped to meet every expectation. A Deluxe horn tank, chrome wheels with whitewall tires, a headlight and a pair of dual carrier racks filled out the order sheet. The Is and IIs were equally fitted, but wore an added dash of chrome as well as Radiant colors of violet, blue and green.

First seen in 1938, the Hollywood reappeared in 1957 as a middleweight model. Listed as "unequipped" on the dealer sheets, it still offered style for the female rider. A wide array of colors was available, and each was more glamorous than the last. Summer Cloud White met with Holiday Rose, and Powder Blue was also partnered with Summer Cloud White. Despite being "unequipped," the Hollywoods sold well. They were not shown in the 1961 catalogs, but were back in 1962. They were sold until 1982.

After a rash of insect and animal nameplates, Schwinn shifted gears and went after natural disasters for inspiration. The Tornado, first introduced for 1958 was aimed at the lower end of the market. "America's Whirlwind Bike Value" was the phrase coined to boost sales of the newly named model. With its price tag of only $39.95, the Tornado held obvious appeal. Being an entry-level model, Tornados were fitted with single-speed coaster brake hubs. Models for girls and boys were sold, in 20-inch, 24-inch and 26-inch sizes. The boys' models were all painted red while the girls' wore blue.

The frame on the boys' bikes featured a pair of parallel frame tubes that were straight versus curved. These bars ran horizontally between the steering head and the seat post.

If you were on a budget but still wanted a bit more bike than the standard Tornado, a Deluxe Tornado rolled onto showrooms for 1959. The Deluxe Tornado cost $10 more than the standard model. It featured a horn tank, headlight and carrier rack. Despite the new gear, the Deluxe rode on the same single-speed hub of the standard model. The 20-inch variety was not offered in the Deluxe range but only the 24-inch and 26-inch. The Tornados blew off the charts in 1961: discontinued.

To fill the void caused by no girls' Corvette models, Schwinn introduced the Debutante in 1959. Fully loaded, the Debutante made quite a splash. Whitewall tires, dual carrier racks along with dual headlights began the parade. A slim line horn tank, two-tone saddle and an intricate seat tube graphic followed up. For the first two years of production only a single-speed hub was available. For the final two years of sales, 1961 and 1962, you could order a two-speed automatic or cable-operated three-speed.

Yet another girls-only machine was introduced in 1959. The Fair Lady was equipped as well as the Debutante, but came standard with a three-speed hub. Other choices included a single or two-speed

Much of the American automotive world was being by passion for the all-new Corvette first introduced in 1953. To capitalize on this fervor, Schwinn named their first middleweight the Corvette.

hub. The Fair Lady carried stainless steel fenders as well. The middleweight Fair Lady was built for only three years: 1959, 1960 and 1961. The name would reappear on the all new girls' Sting-Ray models in 1964.

Never content to sell only one level of bicycle, Schwinn added the Co-Ed to the girls' catalog pages for 1960. Blackwall tires rolled on chrome wheels, but painted fenders and frame kept the bike at a lower level than the other models offered. A Co-Ed could be purchased with a 24-inch or 26-inch frame, except in 1962 when the 24-inch version was not seen. The entire run of the Co-Ed ended in 1964.

The list of middleweight entries was almost endless, but most were merely slight variations on a theme. Spitfire, Bantam, Buddy, Catalina, Flying Star, Fiesta, Heavy-Duti and Barbie are only a few that were sold between 1955 and 1982.

The middleweight machines had carried the load for several years, but a renewed interest in the multi-speed lightweights was beginning to grow. The Paramount had been around since 1938 and still had a list of die-hard buyers, but their numbers were too few to really add any money to the bottom line. What Schwinn needed was a lower-priced lightweight to fill in the hole.

A page from a 1959 Schwinn comic book spoke of the Jaguar as "America's Most Wanted Bicycle."

The ten-speed Continental was the first to be rolled out for 1960. It featured 1-1/4-inch-wide tires and a choice of frame sizes. The smooth-shifting derailleur allowed the rider to find the exact gear needed for any riding condition. Hand-operated caliper brakes on both wheels provided a high level of stopping power on such a light bike.

Another new lightweight for 1960 was the Varsity. The name was resurrected from a lightweight model of the '50s, but the 1960 model was all new. The first year Varsity provided eight speeds and was also available in a variety of frame sizes to best suit the rider. An Ideale racing seat and caliper brakes added to the likeable mix. With a list price of only $69.95, it was an easy choice for the new lightweight rider. The Varsity had an extra two speeds added for the 1961 models. An early problem with the shifting mechanism we corrected when an engineer from Shimano discussed the trouble with Schwinn's Al Fritz over a friendly game of golf. A Shimano-designed component solved the immediate dilemma and opened the door for future transactions with the Japanese company.

Soon after the Varsity and Continental were introduced, other lightweight models were rolled out. The Collegiate, Breeze, Suburban and Super Sport all offered a different twist to the new touring rider.

Tandem bikes had been another small slice of the Schwinn pie, and the addition of the Town and Country Tandem was also made in 1961. Dubbed Model T15, the T&C rolled on 26x1-1/2-inch tires and could be ordered with a three-speed derailleur.

Wowe·e·e... a Schwinn Racer!

Schwinn Bicycles are sold *and Serviced* . . . only by factory-franchised Schwinn Dealers, carefully selected to serve you *and your children* with courtesy and dependability.

Replacement parts and expert service always available through franchised Schwinn Dealers everywhere—see your classified telephone directory.

Every Schwinn Bicycle is made in America and Guaranteed Long-As-You-Own-It.

3-Speed SCHWINN RACER
$49⁹⁵*
SALE PRICE
Regular $56.95*

•
BUDGET TERMS
At Most
SCHWINN DEALERS
•

* Suggested prices, slightly higher South and West. All prices subject to change without notice.

The most exciting moment in a lifetime!

. . . *especially* if it's a real Schwinn, the bike kids all over America know is the best. How proud he'll be on Christmas morning to take that first spin around the block on a sparkling new Schwinn!

Dad will be proud, too—because he knows Schwinn bikes are built better, stronger and safer . . . specially designed to stand up under the rough-and-ready handling of all-American kids.

The Schwinn RACER shown above is Schwinn's newest achievement in sixty years of building fine lightweight bicycles—and at an amazing new low price! Three-speed gears, front and rear hand brakes, all the popular features—*plus* dependable Schwinn quality. See it today!

Over 65 Schwinn models—in every price range

ARNOLD, SCHWINN & COMPANY
CHICAGO 39, ILLINOIS
—*World's Finest Bicycles—Made In America*—

Promoted as a lower-cost alternative to other lightweight machines, the Racer provided a nice blend of features at a reduced cost.

As popular as the line of Schwinn heavyweight and middleweight bikes had been, no one expected new designs to do any better. How wrong they were!

The J-38 Sting-Ray was an all-new model from Schwinn introduced in the middle of 1963. This radical design would soon prove to be a huge success for the company. The black-wall "Nobby" tire on the rear factored into the "Exciting New Riding Thrill."

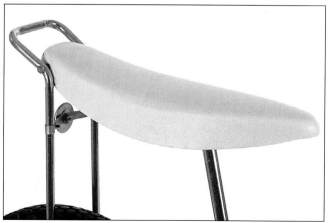

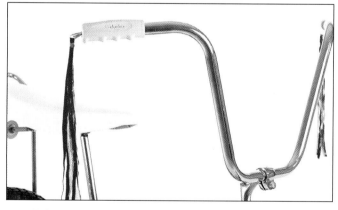

Top left: *Although a fresh design, the Sting-Ray continued the tradition of listing the model name on the chain guard.*

Bottom left: *With the new frame design came a fresh seat style. The Solo Polo saddle was joined by the square-back "sissy bar" and delivered both seating comfort and style.*

Top right: *The high-rise handlebars were another styling trick used on the new Sting-Ray models. This example has been augmented with dealer-added streamers, a popular addition at the time.*

Bill Figatner Collection

The American Deluxe earned its moniker by being assembled with 100% American-made components. The rear carrier, fender-mounted headlight and tank only added to the pride of riding an American.

Barnard's Schwinn

Reverse screen printing on the chain guard made a bold statement about the model you were riding.

The chrome-accented, fender-mounted headlight was replaced by a handlebar-mounted light in 1964. The new light produced more output, but the '63 provided more style.

The first Sting-Rays were first introduced in the middle of 1963 and were an instant success. They were like nothing else on the market at the time, but would soon be copied by nearly every other manufacturer in the bicycle industry. Much like the newest entry from Chevrolet that shared the name,

the Sting-Ray would set the world on fire. It was ultra-cool.

As with many cutting-edge fashion trends, California had already begun customizing bicycles to prefigure the not-yet-released Sting-Ray. By adding a long "banana" seat and higher handlebars

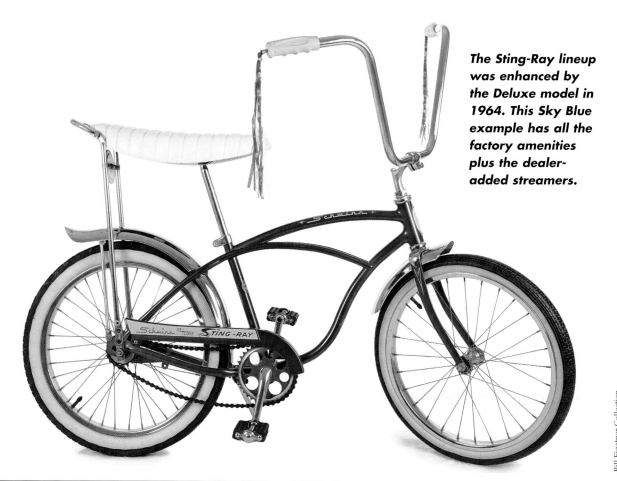

The Sting-Ray lineup was enhanced by the Deluxe model in 1964. This Sky Blue example has all the factory amenities plus the dealer-added streamers.

The Solo Polo seat was still in place, but the Deluxe had the deep tufted surface. Nineteen sixty-four would be the final year for the square back sissy bar. A larger reflector was also seen on the '64 models.

Another obvious identifier on the Deluxe model is the reverse-screen printing on the chain guard.

to existing 20-inch frames, kids were riding the wheels off of these seemingly crazy "pig bike" machines. It turns out that Persons, a well-respected seat maker, had tried to sell the newly-designed banana saddles to the bike market with only limited success. A large inventory sat collecting dust in a warehouse, with little or no commercial interest. The increased demand and resulting shortage of smaller 20-inch frames to build their custom bikes came to the attention of Al Fritz. He had been employed by Schwinn since 1945 and had a seen a few changes in the industry. Sensing a trend about to become a reality, he put pen to paper and began to sketch out the first Sting-Ray models.

Fitted with whitewall tires at both ends, the Deluxe was also trimmed with chrome fenders.

The rear whitewall "Nobby" tire was also covered by a chromed, duck-tail fender.

The J-38 was rolled out in the middle of 1963. Period advertising claimed it was an "Exciting New Riding Thrill!" and touted the list of new "Schwinn Quality Features." Chrome-plated butterfly style handlebars, tubular chrome rims, a Bendix coaster brake and the new Solo Polo Saddle with truss rods were but a few of the highlights shown. The square-back "sissy bar" had a small red reflector attached at the back.

The new model carried a suggested retail price $51.95 in Zone 2 of the Schwinn market. The "sturdy Schwinn 20-inch Cantilever" frame sported a pair of blackwall tires: a 20x1-3/4-inch up front, and 20x2-1/8-inch "Nobby" tire on the back. The application was new, but both rims came from previous models. The S-7 used on the front tire was

This 1964 Deluxe Sting-Ray is finished in a rare shade of Opal Violet.

Beginning in 1964, the designation for Deluxe Sting-Rays was J-39, and the Deluxe model was adorned with many new features and trim. The Sting-Ray seen here is finished in Schwinn Violet.

Bill Figatner Collection

The reverse-screen chain guard was still applied to the newest version of the Deluxe models.

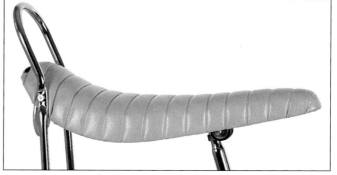

The latest Sting-Ray saddle was the deep-tufted bucket, replacing the solo polo version. This iteration would become a Schwinn trademark. The high-loop sissy bar was another new addition to the Sting-Ray lineup.

used on earlier 20-inch middleweight models while the rear S-2 had held balloon tires on juvenile models. Early Sting-Rays sparkled with 36 spokes on the rear wheel, but that number was reduced to 28 on subsequent models. Front wheels carried 28 spokes from the beginning. Both wheels were fenderless, but no one seemed to complain. Your new Sting-Ray could be purchased in Flamboyant

Red, Flamboyant Lime or Radiant Coppertone.

When creating a new model, Schwinn typically hoped for annual sales of 10,000 units for each fresh variant. Sales of the Sting-Ray approached 50,000 before 1963 was over, and there was no slowing down after the initial fervor was quenched. Had it

The chrome front fender was still in place in 1965, but 1965 two-speed Deluxe models were slowed by a caliper brake on the front wheel.

The dealer signage mounted on the handlebars touted the Deluxe's new features and its list price of $66.95 for the two-speed model.

The Deluxe model came standard with a whitewall "Nobby" tire out back, but the stylish whitewall slick was a popular option. The Deluxe also featured a new two-speed automatic overdrive that was located between the spokes of the rear wheel. The chrome fender was also standard.

not been for a shortage of 20-inch tires, sales would have gone even higher.

The immediate success of the Sting-Ray prompted additional model the very next year. For 1964, a Deluxe Sting-Ray (J39) was offered to the boys, and the all-new (in name only) Fair Lady (J88) was introduced for the girls. The Deluxe Sting-Ray featured chromed front and rear fenders, and a painted chain guard complete with "Deluxe Sting-Ray" emblazoned on the side in reverse screen print. The Solo Polo saddle was now tufted, adding another touch of detail to the rest of the ensemble. A larger reflector was also used on the 1964 square-

back sissy bar. Whitewall tires completed the Deluxe package. New hues of Sky Blue, Radiant Coppertone, and Violet were also added to the options sheet.

The Deluxe model sold for $56.95, $7 higher than the $49.95 Sting-Ray. Colors for the 1964 (J38) Sting-Ray were Flamboyant Lime, Radiant Coppertone, Sky Blue or Flamboyant Red.

The Fair Lady was built for the girls, and featured a step-through frame to permit easier access for skirt-wearing riders. A floral printed basket hung from the bars, and several new colors were available: Blue, Violet and a two-tone combination of white and rose. The Fair Lady was also sold at the $49.95 price point.

First seen in 1964, the Schwinn Twinn Model

Another new offering for 1965 was the Super-Deluxe Sting-Ray. This version is finished in Flamboyant Lime. The Super-Deluxe had all the trimmings of the Deluxe model as well as many other distinct features. Model J36-6s rode on ultra-rare yellow oval blackwall "Sliks".

Bill Figatner Collection

The most obvious addition was the springer front fork. Finished in polished chrome, the suspended front fork brought a new level of comfort to the Sting-Ray, plus a big dose of cool.

T11 tandem was built with a frame that provided easy access to both saddles with its angled top tubes. Schwinn's other tandem, the T10, had a horizontal top bar in the front half of the frame, with a sloping bar in the rear section. Designed for male riders up front, the ladies in the rear, the

Schwinn Twinn was sold in Flamboyant Red and Radiant Blue or White, and either tandem could be ridden home for $99.50.

A new face in the lightweight crowd appeared in 1964 as the five-speed Collegiate. Pitched as a budget-priced derailleur model, the Collegiate featured tourist handlebars and a full-size saddle. This new entry was sold in three frame sizes: 19-inch (C11), 21-inch (C12), and 23-inch (C13) for a meager $56.95 in Flamboyant red, Radiant Blue or Black.

For 1965, Schwinn made a wide variety of alterations and upgrades to the Sting-Ray models. Their sales continued unabated, and new variations only fanned the flames.

The most obvious change was the new saddle. The Solo Polo design was revised to the Deep Tufted Bucket design. Beneath the new saddle

Top left: *A partially chromed chain guard also distinguished the Super-Deluxe different from other Sting-Ray models. Bottom left: A more subtle feature were the large-cap, bow pedals.*

Top right: *By this time standard issue on Sting-Rays, the deep-tufted bucket saddle was first seen on the Super-Deluxe. Bottom right: Fitted with the coaster brake, the Super-Deluxe sold for the same $66.95 as the caliper brake Deluxe model.*

rolled the latest in Schwinn creations, the Slik rear tire. A whitewall Slik could also be ordered, but only in 1965. The standard and Deluxe bikes could be fitted with this radical new rubber, but the Deluxe came stock with a "Nobby" rear tire. The earlier square-back sissy bar was also replaced by the high-loop version. The large reflector remained in place. Another carryover was the reverse screen chain guard first used on the Deluxe 1964 models. Deluxe Sting-Rays for 1965 used a hand-operated caliper brake on the front wheel.

Gear choices for 1965 were many. The standard Sting-Rays could shift with one, two, or three-speed hubs. The two-speed version was the Bendix

Automatic Overdrive, while the three-speed came from Sturmey-Archer and was cable operated. A two-speed Deluxe Sting-Ray, Model J39-1 sold for $66.96 in 1965.

Another entrant in the 1965 Sting-Ray catalog was the Super Deluxe (J36-6 and J37-6) models. By adding a 20-inch springer-fork to the Deluxe chassis, the Super Deluxe was born. It could be bought with the Yellow Oval Slik (J36-6) or a "Nobby" whitewall (J37-6) rear tire, and shift with a single ($68.95) or two-speed ($76.95) hub. The chain guard on the Super Deluxe Sting-Ray was partially chromed, adding another distinction from the other versions.

Another Schwinn for the girls was the Slik Chik. This model is finished in Flamboyant Lime and rides on a yellow-oval, whitewall Slik.

The chain guard was chromed and painted and featured the Slik Chik moniker.

The rarely seen yellow-oval, whitewall Slik. This version of the whitewall Slik was applied to Schwinn bikes only in 1965.

Designed for use by the fairer sex, a handlebar mounted basket seemed appropriate.

The Super-Deluxe was back for another year of fun, and this Radiant Coppertone model is fully trimmed with dealer options. The Silver-Glow saddle was new, and small-cap bow pedals were used to power the bike along.

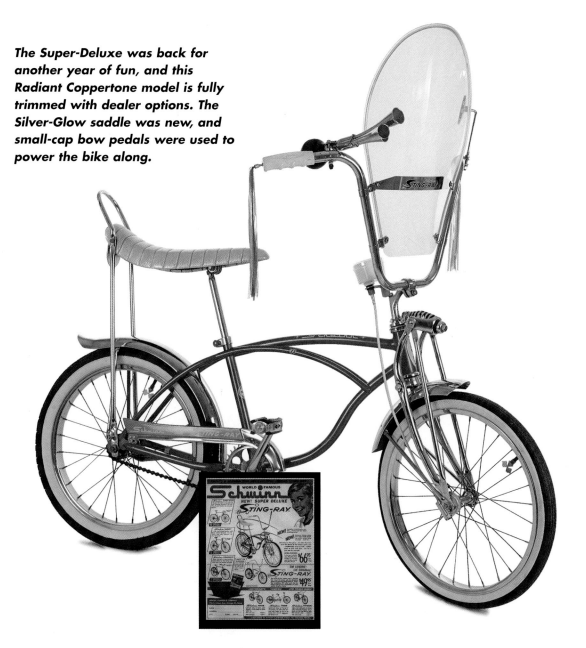

A fourth boys' Sting-Ray variant was the fenderless J33, which came with a blackwall Slik rear tire, and a 20-inch springer front fork. A coaster brake version sold for $58.95 and the Automatic two-speed model went for $66.95. It shared the same style chain guard as the standard Sting-Ray, as well as the bars and saddle. Flamboyant Lime, Radiant Coppertone, Sky Blue and Violet were the color choices.

Smaller enthusiasts had the Junior Sting-Ray (J48) to ride home. Equipped with a polo saddle and short-rise bars, the Junior model allowed those lacking in stature to join in the fun. Chrome fenders added to the Radiant Coppertone, Sky Blue or Violet paint schemes. A paltry $41.95 was all it took to add one to the garage.

For the girls, the Slik Chik (J90) was introduced in 1965. Built with a low contour frame, the Slik Chik was nicely equipped. The whitewall, yellow-oval Slik was the stock rear tire, but only in 1965.

The whitewall Knobby tires rolled on spoked rims, and the crossed-flag stem covers were color matched.

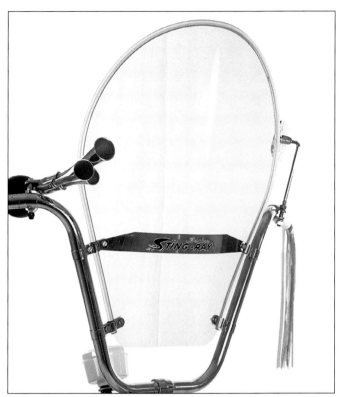

The addition of the Sting-Ray windshield made this example stand out from the crowd.

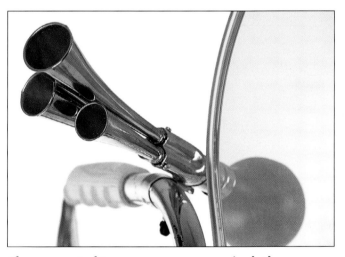

If you wanted to announce your arrival, the Schwinn Triple note horn was the perfect tool for the job.

The colorful basket was part of the factory equipment. The chromed and screened chain guard was also standard. Slik Chik was also sold in coaster brake trim for $58.95 or with an Automatic two-speed for $66.95. Color choices in 1965 were Flamboyant Lime, Radiant Coppertone and Violet.

An improved five-speed Deluxe Twinn (T12) was also shown in the 1965 catalog. The 26-inch model still had a pair of sloping top frame tubes to allow easy mounting and dismounting, regardless of the rider's gender. The Deluxe Twinn retailed for $121.50.

The lightweight class had a few new students as well. The Deluxe Racer for men featured upright handlebars, chrome fenders both front and rear and the latest mattress saddle. The 19-inch model D11 was sold in a coaster brake version ($48.95) or your choice of two or three-speed hubs for $56.95. A larger 21-inch model (D12) was sold with the same

Another themed option: the Checker Board mirror.

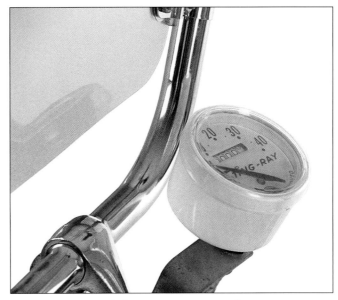

Early versions of the Sting-Ray speedometer were made with white plastic housings, later replaced by metal versions. The plastic model sold for $6.95 in 1968.

choice of gears at the same price as the 19-inch. D13 was a 23-inch version that was available only in the two or three-speed variations at $56.95. For the ladies, the five-speed Collegiate joined the fray. Chrome fenders, mattress saddle and a Sprint derailleur were all utilized on this new bike. Retail priced at $58.95, the Collegiate was offered in only one frame size: 26-inch (#769).

Sting-Ray variations would continue to flourish for 1966, and a new model would also join the ranks.

On the Super Deluxe Sting-Ray, the studded rear tire would become standard, and Flamboyant Lime was removed from the order sheets.

The Tufted, Silver-Glow saddle was first offered and small-cap bow pedals were found on the ends of the crank. The coaster brake model (J37-6) sold for $68.95 and the two-speed overdrive version (J37-1) retailed for $76.95.

The Deluxe Sting-Ray also found the new Tufted Silver-Glow saddle among its standard hardware. The coaster brake model (J39-6) sold for $58.95 and both the three-speed ((J39-4) and two-speed (J39-1) listed at $68.95.

The saddle on the Sting-Ray was upgraded to

The all-new FastBack retailed for $69.95 in 1966 and was advertised alongside several other Schwinn bikes.

The frame of this tandem is stamped with a 1966 build date, but as far as any records indicate it was never a production model. Speculation leads us to believe that it was built to meet a dealer's "special order" request.

Matt Mutchler Collection

The Schwinn name is barely legible on the frame tube, but the diminished appearance and serial number are enough to tell us it was built by the company.

A pair of standard handlebars was mounted to the steering head.

Above: Mattress saddles were in position for both riders, and the rear bars reached higher to accommodate the back-seat driver.

Left: The chain guard is adorned with nothing more than a simple pinstripe instead of the typical model name being screen printed there.

A Deluxe Sting-Ray is shown here in Campus Green.

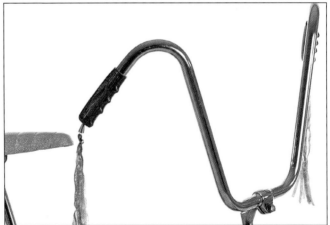

Top left: *The painted and screened chain guard is standard on the Deluxe models.*

Bottom left: *The Deluxe Sting-Rays were offered with the two-speed rear hub.*

Top right: *The widely spaced handlebars were used until they were replaced by the "safer" narrow-spaced versions.*

Bill Figatner Collection

Another variation in the Sting-Ray family was the Fastback. Even more exotic was the Ram's Horn Fastback version. Narrow 20-inch tires at both ends helped set the Fastback apart from the other Sting-Rays available. The "rat-trap" pedals were all steel, with sharp edges to keep your feet on the pedals. They were later eliminated due to injuries sustained from riders hurting themselves on the sharp edges.

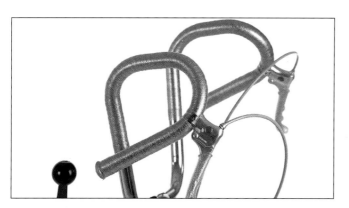

Top left: *The handlebars made all the difference on this model and added another distinctive touch to the Sting-Ray lineage.*

Bottom left: *The Ram's Horn theme was carried out on the screened chain guard, too.*

Top right: *The five-speed Fastback was shifted using the 8-ball lever mounted to the top of the frame. The same shift lever would later appear on the 1968 Krate bikes.*

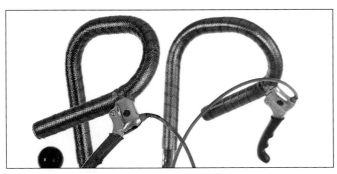

The second and final year of the Ram's Horn Fastback model was 1968. This one is finished in Sky Blue and has the rat-trap pedals that were used on both years of the bike's production.

The bars made all the difference, and while they set the Ram's Horn model apart from the rest, sales of the model were never brisk enough to keep it in the catalog.

the new Silver-Glow smoothie for 1966 as well. Prices increased to $51.95 for the coaster brake (J38-6), and $61.95 for the three-speed (J38-4) and two-speed (J38-1) versions. In 1966 Sting-Rays saw the first use of the standard low loop sissy bar.

To compliment the Junior Sting-Ray introduced in 1965 for the boys, the Lil Chik (J81-6) appeared in 1966 for the girls. The dropped tube frame, short-rise bars and polo saddle were attached to a Radiant Sky Blue or Violet frame and sold for $41.95.

An entirely new iteration of the Sting-Ray was the Fastback model. A mildly curved top frame bar and the lack of the cantilever bars led to the final name choice, as directed by Al Fritz, the Sting-Ray's creator.

The 1966 Fastbacks were built using French-made Sprint derailleurs, hubs and sprockets. The 1966 models also rolled on a pair of matching 20x1-3/8-inch tires. From 1967 and beyond, they sported a 20x 1-3/8-inch tire up front and a Slik out back and had a "MAG" sprocket and American-made components.

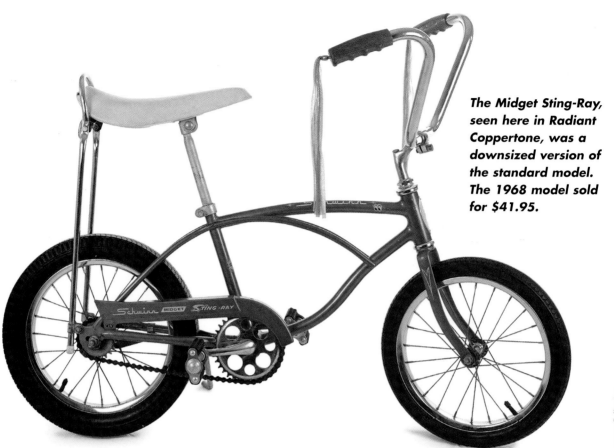

The Midget Sting-Ray, seen here in Radiant Coppertone, was a downsized version of the standard model. The 1968 model sold for $41.95.

Above: *As always, the chain guard indicates the model designation.*

Right: *The 16-inch rim at the rear end was wrapped with a Gripper Slik tire.*

1968 was the first year for the new line of Krate models from Schwinn. Based on the popular Sting-Ray, the Krate added several features making it the coolest ride on the street. A fenderless front wheel marks the '68 models from the rest.

The Stik-Shift, mounted on the curved upper frame tube, allowed the rider to row through five speeds via a derailleur with 37 to 74 gearing. The "eight-ball" atop the Stik-Shift lever was embossed with a circled "5" to tell the world what you had. In 1966, the handlebars were altered to a new swept-back drop-down design that was fitting for the new model. Chrome fenders protected the rider from debris at both ends of the bike. The now standard deep tufted saddle looked right at home on the Fastback.

All new small-cap bow pedals were incorporated onto the early Fastback models, but were later replaced with a more common Schwinn design. Black, Violet, Sky Blue and Radiant Coppertone were on tap in 1966.

A new middleweight model with a previously-used name also rolled in for 1966. The Starlet III (B67-6) came equipped with chrome fenders and carrier racks at both ends, and its slim-line tank held the built-in horn. Schwinn Superior nylon whitewall tires were complemented by Radiant Sky Blue or Violet paint. Sold only in coaster brake form, the Starlet carried a price tag of $59.95.

Sensing a shift towards people wanting to get fit in America, Schwinn introduced their first at-home exercise machines in 1966. The Schwinn Exerciser (XR1) was only the tip of the iceberg when it came to home fitness, but it was a great place for Schwinn to position itself for coming years.

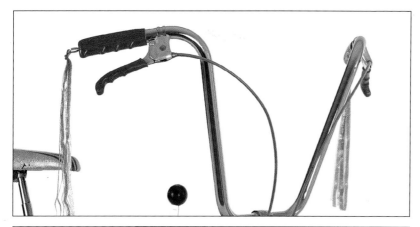

Top left: *The widely spaced bars would be changed on the 1970 models to meet government safety criteria.*

Top right: *One of the neatest features was the frame-mounted shift lever. Early versions of the Krate bike had these solid shifters with a top-mounted knob. The 8-ball shifter appeared only on the 1968 Krate bikes.*

Bottom left: *On the rear end, the Krates wore a pair of shock absorbers, adding a bit of comfort and a lot of cool.*

Above: *The Orange Line Knobby rear tire on the Krate was the factory installed tire in the early part of 1968. By the time the other Krates had arrived in the middle of 1968, Color Line Sliks were installed on the series.*

On the first day of January, 1967 the Arnold, Schwinn Company became the Schwinn Bicycle Company. Still under the same family control, it seemed fitting to relinquish the secondary founder's name to begin a new era.

Changes to the Sting-Ray group continued but were more subtle in 1967. The Sting-Ray now carried Fastback drop-down design handlebars and could be had with a trigger-controlled three-speed hub. Four models of Sting-Ray were seen in 1967: coaster brake (J38-6) $51.95; two-speed overdrive (J38-1) $61.95; three-speed trigger control (J38-4) $61.95; and three-speed with frame-mounted Stik-Shift (J38-3) $68.95.

The Deluxe Sting-Ray was seen in coaster brake (J39-6) trim ($60.95); two-speed overdrive with a

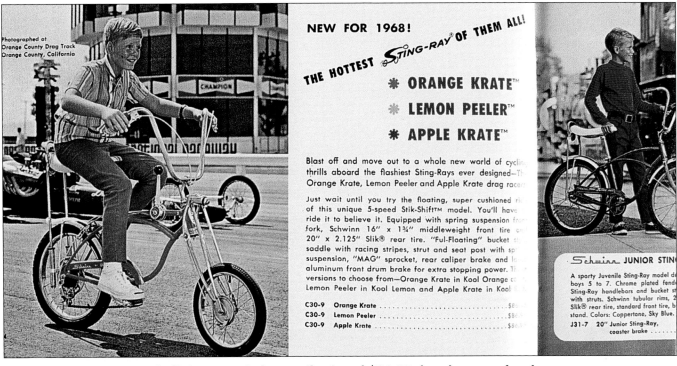

Photographed at
Orange County Drag Track
Orange County, California

NEW FOR 1968!

THE HOTTEST *Sting-Ray* OF THEM ALL!

* ORANGE KRATE™
* LEMON PEELER™
* APPLE KRATE™

Blast off and move out to a whole new world of cycling thrills aboard the flashiest Sting-Rays ever designed—The Orange Krate, Lemon Peeler and Apple Krate drag racers.

Just wait until you try the floating, super cushioned ride of this unique 5-speed Stik-Shift™ model. You'll have to ride it to believe it. Equipped with spring suspension front fork, Schwinn 16" x 1¾" middleweight front tire and 20" x 2.125" Slik® rear tire. "Ful-Floating" bucket seat saddle with racing stripes, strut and seat post with spring suspension, "MAG" sprocket, rear caliper brake and large aluminum front drum brake for extra stopping power. Three versions to choose from—Orange Krate in Kool Orange color, Lemon Peeler in Kool Lemon and Apple Krate in Kool Red.

C30-9	Orange Krate	$86.95
C30-9	Lemon Peeler	$86.95
C30-9	Apple Krate	$86.95

Schwinn JUNIOR STING

A sporty Juvenile Sting-Ray model designed for boys 5 to 7. Chrome plated fenders, Sting-Ray handlebars and bucket style with struts. Schwinn tubular rims, 20" Slik® rear tire, standard front tire, band stand. Colors: Coppertone, Sky Blue.

J31-7 20" Junior Sting-Ray, coaster brake . . . .

"The hottest Sting-Ray of all time" carried a retail price of $86.95, but the entry fee drove many youngsters to work extra hard to earn their new machine.

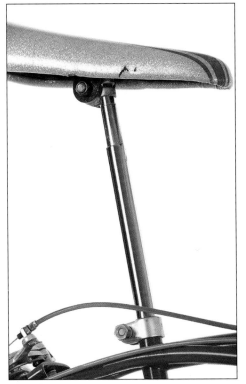

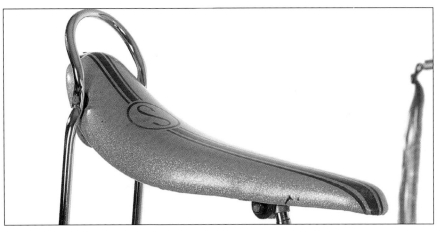

Above: The 1968 Krate bikes were the only ones to wear a silver-glow saddle with contrasting trim. Subsequent models would be fitted with a saddle wrapped in vinyl to match the color of the bike.

Left: A full-floating, sprung seat post was seen only on the 1968 Krate models. The combination of the rear shocks and the pogo-style seat post gave the Krates a fully floating saddle. 1968/04C The front fork on the Krates was complete with a coil spring for comfort. The five-speed models also claimed a front drum brake.

single handbrake (J39-1) ($77.95); and the three-speed Stik-Shift (J39-3) with a pair of hand brakes ($77.95).

The Fastback was again seen in the catalog and now retailed for $71.95. The Mag sprocket and rear Slik were now standard equipment.

Providing an even higher degree of style, the Fastback could also be purchased in the Ram's

The Orange Krate seen here was the 1 millionth unit built by Schwinn in 1968. It had taken the company until 1916 to build the first million bikes. For some reason, this 1968 model has a 1969 shifter and dealer-added saddle.

Left: *This company portrait shows the lucky Krate along with many of the proud factory workers who assembled it, and many more like it, that year.*

Horn variation in 1967. The rolling stock was all the same as the standard Fastback, but the Ram's Horn carried a twisted set of handlebars that really stood out from the other Sting-Ray models. The Ram's Horn Fastbacks were sold only in 1967 and 1968 before slipping off the charts. The all-steel rat-trap pedals were used on both years of the Ram's Horn's availability.

For the entry level Sting-Ray rider, the Midget Sting-Ray (J48-7) was built on a miniature cantilever frame, and hit the streets on a pair of 16-inch tires.

For families with boys and girls, the convertible model would satisfy the needs of both flavors of beginning riders. By removing the top frame tube,

This 1968 Sting-Ray is a fenderless, 2-speed model in Sky Blue.

all of these smaller Schwinns could be ridden by the girls in the crowd. The upper tube could just as easily be replaced when boys stepped up for a ride. The Bantam model was a 20-inch version, and was styled closer to a middleweight than a Sting-Ray. Bantams wore whitewall tires and chrome fenders on both wheels.

Left: *The fenderless model allowed unobstructed views of the blackwall Slik.*

Right: *Although not a Krate bike, a Sting-Ray could be equipped with a twin shock absorber suspension.*

Above left: *By turning the vertical lever to loosen the clamp, the seat post could be lowered into the frame of the bike, then pulled out again when it was time to ride. Right: A matching lever was placed on the handlebar mount to allow the bars to be lowered against the frame.*

A Deluxe Exerciser (XR3) was also added to the lineup in 1967. A frame-mounted control panel showed the rider both speed and mileage from the comfort of the adjustable saddle.

Although the Ram's Horn model disappeared in 1968, Schwinn's newest product would make us all forget about the poor-selling Ram. Combining all the greatest options found on the other Sting-Rays, and turning up the heat a few notches, the Krate bikes were born. First to be released was the Orange Krate Model C30-9, and it was like nothing seen before.

The frame, handlebars and saddle were basically the same as on the other Sting-Ray models,

Above: *Many features on the Run-A-Bout were full-sized, such as the sprocket and chain guard.*

First sold in 1968, the Run-A-Bout featured folding handlebars and an adjustable seat to allow the rider to easily stow the bike away when not being ridden.

Sold for one year only, the Mini-Twinn offered a "sporty" ride in a bicycle built for two in 1968. Twenty-inch wheels kept both riders close to the ground.

Matt Mutchler Collection

The rider seated up front grabbed a pair of high-rise bars shared by the Sting-Ray model.

but a raft of new appointments set the Krates apart.

The front 24-inch fork now came equipped with a functional spring, providing a new level of comfort to the rider. A fenderless 16x1-3/4-inch middleweight Superior front tire was wrapped around a spoked wheel. An Atom drum brake was located within the front hub, delivering a higher level of deceleration.

The 20x2-1/8-inch rear Orange Color-Line "Nobby" tire sat in a spoked rim, and a chrome fender kept the rider's backside dry. The saddle was shaped the same as on the other Sting-Rays but sported a racing stripe and Schwinn "S" logo. In 1968 Krate saddles were finished in silver-glow vinyl and were trimmed with a racing stripe to match the model chosen. The front pogo-seat post of the 1968 Krate bikes was also sprung, but none of the subsequent years would have this feature.

All Krate machines carried the twin shocks on the rear of the seat. The result of the sprung post and twin shocks was a "Ful-Floating" bucket style saddle. The rear wheel was fitted with a caliper brake, operated by the hand lever mounted on the wide-spaced handlebars.

A five-speed Stik-Shift was mounted on the

Pictured in the Schwinn catalog for 1968 was a happy couple aboard what was destined to become a rare Schwinn collector's item.

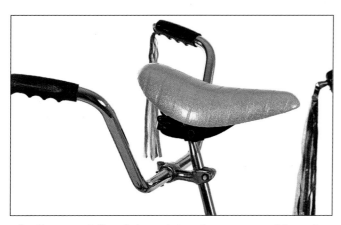

The front saddle of the Mini Twinn was positioned between the low-rise bars of the rear rider and was the only Schwinn ever to use this seat.

With power delivered through both sprockets, a tensioner was on board to keep the chain from flailing around. The extra-long chain guard kept things tidy.

The rear passenger rested on a full-scale banana seat, another item from the Sting-Ray parts bin.

upper frame tube, and for 1968 only they were topped off with the eight-ball, five-speed knob. The lever was flat and without any bends but had some horizontal serrations scribed into the steel.

The Orange Krate was the first model rolled out, and it was followed mid-year by the Lemon Peeler and Apple Krate. Kool Orange, Kool Lemon and Flamboyant Red were the official color designations for these first Krates.

With the Krates' retail price of $86.95, Schwinn could barely build them fast enough to meet

The 1969 Krates were altered in several ways from the premier 1968 models, but their popularity was growing without hesitation. The Lemon Peeler was sold in the latter part of 1968, and returned for another year in 1969.

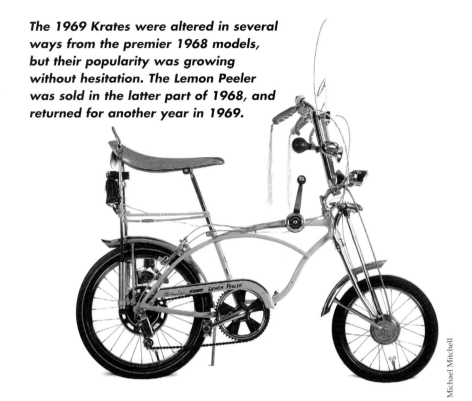

Michael Mitchell

The shift lever and knob was one of three variations used during the 1969 model year. The nearly 90-degree bend at the top of the lever and the gentle "S" at the bottom were topped off by the black knob that was devoid of any gear number. This is the first version used for that year.

The rear Gripper Slik color line tire was new for 1969 and would also be a single-year item for the Krates. Buffed and lettered blackwall Sliks were used the following year.

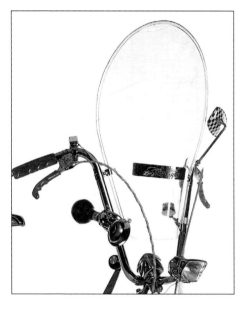

The official Sting-Ray windshield kept the rider safe from inclement weather but did little to enhance aerodynamics.

demand. For the first time ever, in 1968, with the help of the Krate bikes, Schwinn sold in excess of one million bikes in a single year. It had taken the company from 1895 to 1916 to sell their first million units in total. An Orange Krate was THE millionth unit sold in 1968 alone, and the bike became a centerpiece for Schwinn propaganda.

There was no lack of new models in 1968, and most were based somewhat on the popular Sting-ray line. The Run-A-Bout offered a rider a way to carry his Schwinn in the trunk until it was time to ride. No tools were required to lower the saddle into the seat tube and fold the handlebars flat against the upper frame tube. Once compressed, it

CHWINN "KRATES"

Schooner Bay General Store

GENERAL STORE

PRESCRIPTIONS
SOUVENIRS
HARDWARE
GOODS
BAKERY

NEW FOR 1969!

Schwinn

Krates

- ORANGE KRATE®
- LEMON PEELER®
- APPLE KRATE®
- PEA PICKER®

A whole new world of cycling thrills can be yours when you blast off and move out aboard the flashiest Sting-Rays ever designed — The Orange Krate, Lemon Peeler, Apple Krate and Pea Picker drag racers from Schwinn.

Just wait until you try the floating, super cushioned ride of this swift 5-speed Stik-Shift model. Equipped with spring suspension front fork, Schwinn 16" x 1¾" middleweight front tire and 20" x 2.125" Gripper Slik® Color line rear tire, bucket style saddle with rally stripes, chrome plated fenders, patented spring strut, "MAG" sprocket, rear caliper brake and large aluminum drum brake. Colors: Orange Krate in Kool Orange, Lemon Peeler in Kool Lemon, Apple Krate in Kool Red and Pea Picker in Kool Green.

C30-9	Orange Krate	..........$91.95
C30-9	Lemon Peeler	..........$91.95
C30-9	Apple Krate	..........$91.95
C30-9	Pea Picker	..........$91.95

Schwi

STI

THE BIKE

Sting-Ray, known as has revolutionized cy in 1963. It has wor tion of youngsters of fun bike that feature and long, bucket sha an exciting combina fast starts and short

A lightweight versio was introduced in 19 This is the 5-speed of a lightweight wit Sting-Ray. It also ac tion of 5-speed gears For distance rides, the Schwinn Fastbac

in 1968, Schwinn op ment with the unv Orange Krate Sting-Stik-Shift model has in "bikedom." This sions of the Krate li feature the combina front wheel, with sty drag racing tracks.

The Krate family was joined by the Pea Picker in 1969, finished in Campus Green with matching seat. Retail prices went up by $5 to $91.95.

could be placed into a small space and set up upon arrival. Sixteen-inch whitewall tires were used at both ends, and selection of the three-speeds could be done with a trigger control or Stik Shift model. Chrome fenders and a choice of Campus Green or Sierra Brown finished off the list. The trigger shift version sold for $64.95 and the Stik Shift went for $5 more.

Another fresh face in the 1968 catalog was the Mini-Twinn. Complete with Sting-Ray inspired styling, the Mini-Twinn kept a low profile by riding on a pair of 20" whitewall tires. A full size Sting-Ray

The girls' Hollywood made a simple fashion statement and provided a comfortable mount for rides into Tinseltown, or anywhere else you chose to travel.

The two-tone basket and battery powered headlight were both popular options for the Hollywood and other Schwinn bikes.

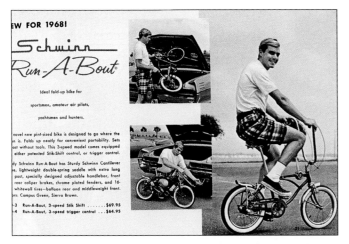

Offered in 1968, 1969, and 1970, the first models were also available with a three-speed Stik-Shift and whitewall tires.

To make sure people knew what you were riding as you made your entrance, the chain guard called out the Hollywood name clearly.

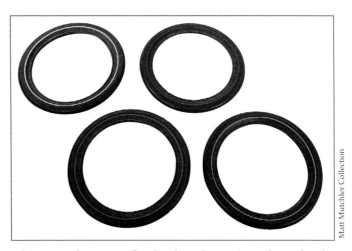

This complete set of color-line front tires dates back to 1969 when they were first offered. An exciting option at the time, they have become the holy grail of collectors.

Matt Mutchler Collection

bucket was home for the rear rider while a reduced version was the lead rider's perch. A coaster brake model was $99.50, and the automatic two-speed variant sold for $107.50. Other tandem models for 1968 included the Twinn and Deluxe Twinn.

For even smaller riders, or perhaps circus clowns, the Lil Tigers were built on a diminutive frame and wore a 12-inch semi-pneumatic "hard" tire at the front and back. They would stay in the lineup until 1980. The later editions of the Lil

Tiger's chain guards came complete with screened-on warning of "no brakes," forcing the tiny rider to find other means of stopping his new mount. These models were also convertible for boys and girls.

Not every Schwinn model had two or three wheels, as evidenced by the arrival of the Unicycle in 1968. This one-wheeled model was available in 20-inch (U20) or 24-inch (U24) wheel sizes. The saddle was designed to add control and comfort for the rider perched on top. Both models sold for $39.95 in 1968.

Top left: *The chrome and painted chain guard was standard fare for the Krates.*

Top right: *The frame-mounted "Stik-Shift" remained a popular feature on the Krate models. Nineteen-seventy was the first year for the flat-topped "barrel" shift knob mounted to a straighter and slotted shift lever. Gone was the 90-degree bend at the top.*

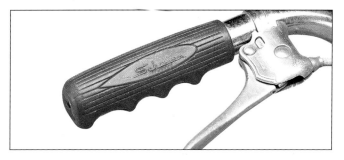

Color-keyed trim pieces remained the standard on many Schwinn bikes, especially the Krates.

For those riders who needed a bit more stability in their lives, the Town & Country adult tri-wheeler was introduced. The three-wheeled model carried a capacious basket complete with carrying handles between its rear tires, and was offered in coaster brake ($136.95) and automatic two-speed ($144.95) variations.

While the new Krates were stealing most of the limelight in 1968, Schwinn still offered a wide variety of mounts, including four different Paramount models, fendered and fenderless Varsity Sports, five different Collegiates, Breeze and Deluxe Breeze, Racer, Deluxe Racer and the Speedster.

For 1969, the Krate family grew by one with the additional of the Pea Picker in Campus Green. All 1969 Krates wore a small, chromed front fender where there had been none in 1968. The solid shift lever also changed three times during the year. The first variation had a slight bend at the bottom and a 90-degree bend at the top.

This version of the lever was finished off with a new knob design that that was somewhat ovoid, but was not stamped with the number "5." A plain silver disc filled the void in the knob. The second iteration had the same shift lever, but it was topped off with a flat-topped, barrel shaped knob with only a silver insert in the recess in the end. The third and final version for the year added another slight bend to the lever near the top, but it was finished off with the same barrel knob.

The FastBack first appeared in 1966 and would share several features with the popular Krate models.

Bicycle Museum of America

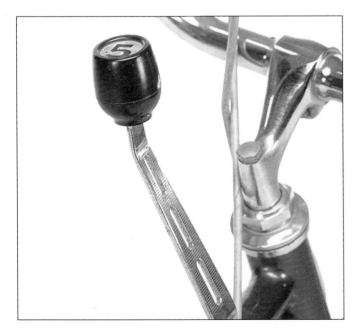

Early versions of the FastBack had a straight shift lever with a black ball knob at the top. This 1970 example carried an "S"-shaped, slotted version with a flat-topped knob. The number "5" was placed into the top of the knob.

In typical Schwinn fashion, the chain guard was emblazoned with the model name.

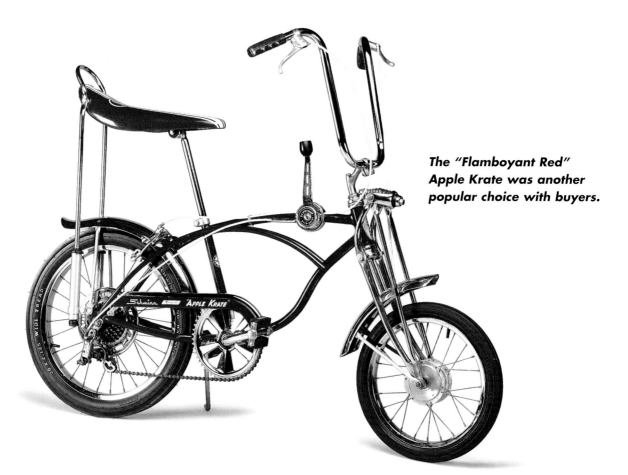

The "Flamboyant Red" Apple Krate was another popular choice with buyers.

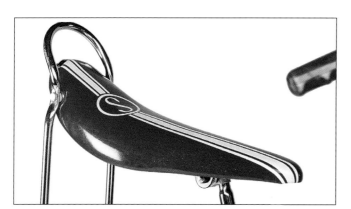

The red vinyl that covered the seat really added some zing to the scheme.

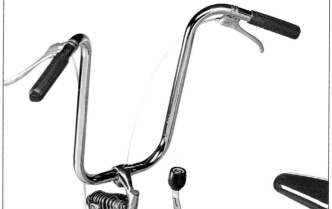

Handlebars remained narrow to address earlier safety concerns of the wide-set bars.

The rear tires on the Krates were now the Color-Line Gripper variety, but for only one year. These tires were sold with a single orange, red, green or yellow band depending on which model of Krate you bought. If you were feeling crazy, you could always put a contrasting color-line tire on

your machine. Introduced later in the model year as an accessory were the front color-line tires to match the rear mounted rubber. Raised white letter (RWL) Sliks would become the standard rubber in 1970. Also in 1969, all Sting-Ray models including the

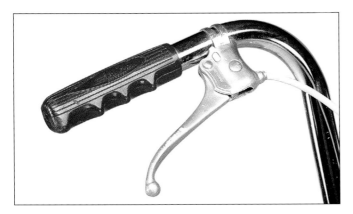

Matching red grips were used at each end of the high-rise handlebars.

Side-pull caliper brakes on the rear wheels were standard on all five-speed Krate models, except for the 1972 and 1973 disc-brake Krates and Manta-Rays.

As was the case since the early days of Schwinn, the name of the bike was printed on the chain guard.

Krates were fitted with color-matching saddles that accented the frame. Another change for all 1969 Schwinn bikes was the new safety/rolled edge fenders. These replaced the depleted supply of razor edge fenders. Suggested retail price for the Krate models went up to $91.95, regardless of color.

The Stardust model was introduced as a girls' version of the Fastback. These models were built with the step-through frame to ease access.

The small 44-tooth MAG type sprocket was used on the girls' models, but they had the added bonus of a detachable basket. These white-laced baskets were trimmed with a row of plastic flowers, and made a nice handbag when removed from the

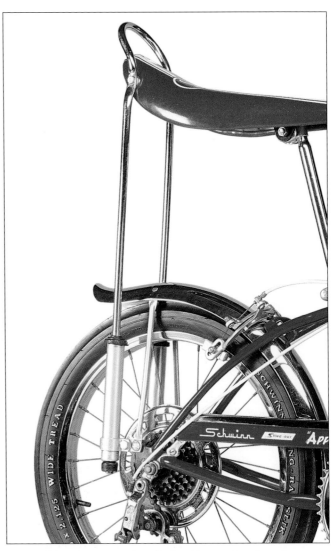

Seated high above the ducktail rear fender, the Krate rider was suspended with a pair of shock absorbers.

Beginning in 1970, not every Krate bike, not even the Cotton Picker, was delivered with the 5-speed Stik Shift. This coaster brake model sold for about $20 less than the 5-speed variants.

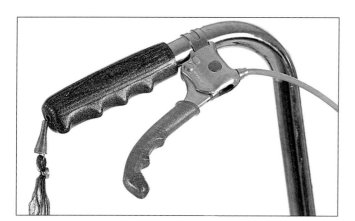

Another option seen here were the color-matched brake lever covers.

The chain guard made no mention of this being a coaster brake version but still called out the Cotton Picker name.

bike. Offered in a coaster brake model for $61.95 and a three-speed version for $71.95. Campus Green, Sky Blue and Violet were the available hues, and each choice came with a saddle finished in a matching shade.

For Tandem riders who demanded and could

afford the best, the Paramount Tandems were released in 1969 as well. Built to the same exacting standards as the solo mount models, the tandems offered performance for two.

The Paramount tandem was available in a

Whatever money the owner saved by purchasing the lower-priced coaster brake model was spent on accessorizing this model. The baseball bat carrier was only the beginning of add-ons.

The official Sting-Ray tail light was battery powered and sold for $2.49.

The Lock and Tool Bag was constructed of "black vinyl cloth" and sold for $1.39.

Up front, the battery powered Deluxe Ball Light lit the way after dark. Complete with "lighted amber side reflectors" it sold for $3.95.

double men's frame (T22), or a men's front, rear step-through version (T19). Your new tandem Paramount could be finished in every Schwinn color. Both frame styles were listed at $395 for 1969.

The year 1970 marked the Diamond Jubilee anniversary for Schwinn and saw the entry of another Krate option, the Cotton Picker. Finished in a simple white paint scheme, the Cotton Picker never had the same appeal as the Krates finished in the "Kool" colors. It would only be sold for two years, 1970 and 1971. The Cotton Picker brought the total of Krate (C30) models to five in 1970.

The Deluxe electric horn was also battery powered and sold for $1.99, which was $.50 more than the simpler electric horn model.

In the event the batteries went dead on your Deluxe electric horn, this Deluxe Ding-Dong bell was on duty to warn those around you. Featuring a Schwinn Approved seal, it sold for $1.95.

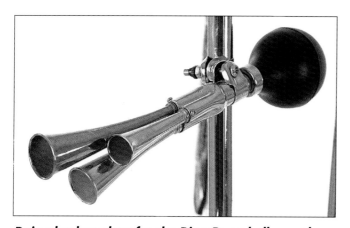

Doing backup duty for the Ding-Dong bell was the Triple note chrome bulb horn. Rack up another $3.95 in the options column.

The Stik Shift lever was once again changed for 1970 models. The lever itself was bent into a mild "S" and was now slotted. The shift knob itself was still a flat-topped barrel design, but now sat upright. The number of speeds, screen-printed onto an aluminum disc, was then pressed into the recessed surface on the top of the knob. Lowering the fun factor, early Sting-Rays including the Krate models were all fitted with narrow-spaced handlebars for the first time in 1970.

The early, openly splayed bars made a perfect perch for a second rider, even though that was not the intended purpose. In an effort to stanch future accidents received by the bar-mounted "passenger," the upright section of the bars was pulled closer together on the 1970 models, eliminating the obvious though unintended perch. Maybe this move was an attempt to get the previous passengers to get their own Schwinns?

A new "deeper, roomier" bucket seat was applied, as was the latest buffed and lettered 20x2-1/8-inch rear Slik tire. The new deeper bucket saddles were also mounted to the Fastback, Sting-Ray and Deluxe Sting-ray models.

With the cost of a five-speed Stik-Shift Krate bike reaching $96.95 by 1970, a single-speed, coaster brake model joined the fray. Although it could be purchased for only $78.95, it lacked the frame-mounted shift lever, taking away from the fun factor. The coaster brake models also lacked a front drum brake, leaving the rear wheel coaster to fill the deceleration duties.

Sold for one year only, the Grey Ghost has become a popular item among collectors. Finished in a metallic Silver-Mist Grey paint, this Krate had an air of elegance.

Blue Moon Bikes Ltd.

Above: The original Grey Ghost chain guard has a drooping front portion of the "S" in "Ghost." Screen printing rather than decals were used on Schwinn chain guards.

Bottom right: Black hand grips finished off the complimentary color scheme.

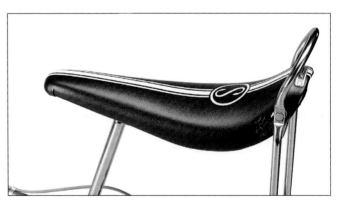

To offset the silver paint, the banana seat was covered in black vinyl.

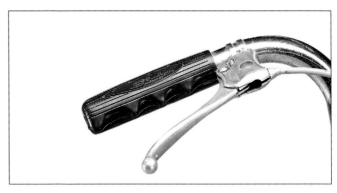

In an attempt to sell Sting-Rays to the older buyer, the Manta-Ray rolled on 24-inch tires. Side-pull brakes at both ends on the five-speed models in 1971 added a higher level of braking power. The Manta-Ray was sold only in 1971 and 1972. The 1972 five-speed models were sold with a rear wheel disc brake.

Bicycle Museum of America

For added comfort, the Manta-Ray seat swelled in the center to carry the added heft of an older rider.

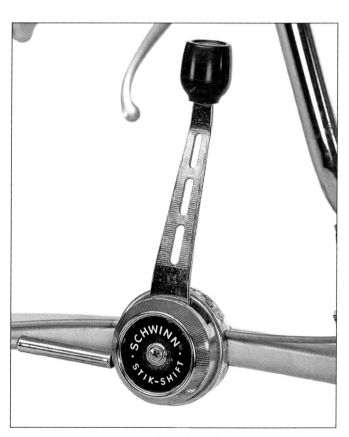

Bringing a touch of cool to the table, the bigger Manta-Ray still came equipped with the "Stik-Shift" unless it was a coaster brake, single-speed version.

The Sting-Ray was available in a myriad of configurations, such as this 1971, 3-speed Stik Shift.

Bill Figatner Collection

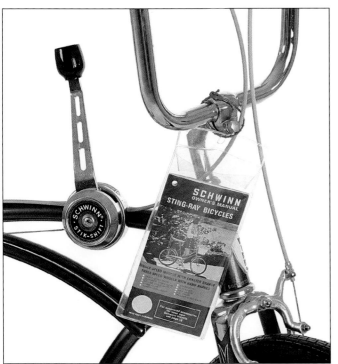

The front caliper brake, original owner's manual and 3-speed Stik shift can all be seen here.

The "Stik Shift" designation was added to the standard Sting-Ray nomenclature on the chain guard.

The same shift lever and flat-topped ball were used, but a "3" took the place of the "5" on the 3-speed versions.

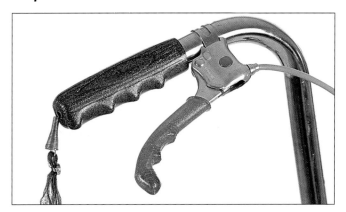

Another option seen here were the color-matched brake lever covers.

A caliper brake was also found on the rear wheel, assisting the front brake when rapid slowing was required.

The 75th anniversary catalog saw the addition of the Suburban line of lightweight models. A diamond-style frame, tubular front fork and choice of ten, five or three-speeds delivered a lot of variety to the new buyers. Three different frame sizes for the men also allowed for a custom fit.

The three-speed hub models carried 52 to 92 gears and sold for $79.95 in 19-inch (419-4), 21-inch (421-4) and 23-inch (423-4) versions. For $81.95, the five-speed model with 39 to 89 gearing came in 19-inch (519-9), 21-inch (521-9) and 23-inch (523-9) iterations. Your third and final options were in the ten-speed, 38:100 gear column and would set you back $86.95; 19-inch (619-9), 21-inch (621-9)

and 23-inch (623-9) were all listed. Regardless of frame size, speeds or gearing, Sierra Brown, Black, Campus Green and Sky Blue were the available colors.

Ladies' models were also seen but provided only 19-inch and 21-inch frame choices. Three, five and ten-speed gearing was still a choice for the female rider.

An even smaller convertible model, the Sting-Ray Pixie (J43-7) was new for 1970. The 16-inch semi-pneumatic tires carried the Campus Green, Red or Violet frame out of the store for $43.95.

Only one indoor Schwinn was seen in 1970 with the removal of the standard Exerciser, leaving the

The three-speed Racer sold for $66.95 in the 1971 catalog and was one of many lightweight options for the Schwinn shopper.

Schwinn side-pull caliper brakes were used on both wheels of the Racer, allowing the rider to go fast and stop safely on his new machine.

A simple chain guard was used on the Racer but still displayed the bike's model name.

Deluxe the only model at $84.95.

For 1971, several new entries were made into the Schwinn catalog.

In the Krate camp, the one-year-only Grey Ghost appeared. Finished in Silver Mist Grey paint, and trimmed with a black saddle and grips, the Grey Ghost added a touch of elegance to the lineup. A total of six different Krates were now available, and the five-speed versions sold for $104.95 while the coasters rolled out at $85.95 a copy.

For bigger Sting-Ray riders, a new departure from the Krate bikes was offered. The Manta-Ray

Upright "Tourist" style handlebars allowed the rider to sit in a more comfortable stance when aboard the Racer.

(H26-9) was built with a Sting-Ray Fastback style frame, but touted a pair of 24-inch tires on both ends. This placed the seat height up where larger riders could feel more at home.

The Manta-Ray was sold for only two years beginning in 1971. Silver Mist was one of the colors offered that year. Manta-Rays came in both five-speed and coaster brake models.

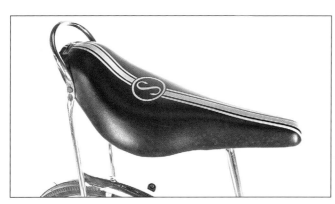

The distended center section of the Manta-Ray saddle was intended to provide extra comfort for the rider.

The typical Sting-Ray saddle was found with a swollen midsection, adding more comfort to the equation as well. Colors in 1971 included Kool Orange, Kool Lemon, Campus Green and Silver Mist. Both five-speed and coaster brake models were sold, and the five-speeds carried a price tag of $92.95.

One minor detail on the 1971 Sting-Ray models was the reflectors in the pedals. Early 1971 models had white reflectors embedded into the sides, and subsequent versions had amber plastic to enhance visibility. This change was applied industry-wide for the safety of riders.

More lightweight choices were made available with the entry of the Sports Tourer model. This new twist on the lightweight design carried ten speeds, and shifted through a Campagnolo Gran Turismo rear derailleur. This offered a gear range between 28:104.

Three different frame sizes were on tap: 22-inch (832), 24-inch (834) and 26-inch (836). All retailed for $199.00. In the paint department, Silver Mist, Lemon, Orange, Sierra Brown and Burgundy were the choices.

RMANCE

VARSITY® SPORT

nn has designed a new
nn Quality Features as
rills and excitement of
wing boy. Take a look
ht frame, drop handle-
rs, dual position caliper
hift controls—up front
ed racing saddle. No
so much . . . no other
s: Kool Lemon, Sierra

T............ $89.95*

ge without notice.

Schwinn MANTA-RAY™

Feature packed from front to rear, the 24" Manta-Ray has never been
equalled for excitement. Now, on 5-speed models, genuine automobile
type disc brakes! Camelback frame, Sting-Ray style saddle, 52 tooth MAG
Sprocket. Choice of colors: Kool Orange, Kool Lemon, or Campus Green.

Model H26-6 Coaster brake Manta-Ray .... $ 69.95*
Model H26-9 5-speed Manta-Ray $101.95*

Schwinn KRATES

The famous Schwinn Sting-Ray design customized with an array of special
high-performance features! Full floating ride with shock absorbing saddle
and front fork, choice of gears, bucket seat, front drum brake. Rear disc
brake on 5-speed models. Choice of colors: Orange Krate, Lemon Peeler,
Apple Krate (red), Pea Picker (green).

C30-6—Coaster brake Krate .... $ 82.95*
C30-9 5-Speed Stik-shift Krate $113.95*
*All prices and specifications subject to change without notice.

NEW! DISC BRAKES ON THESE 5-SPEED MODELS

NEW FOR '72

Inspired by the brakes on
the finest sports cars, the
handlever controls a pow-
erful vise like grip on the
steel disc for sure, safe
stops. Another safety first
for bicycles.

Both Krates and Manta-Rays could be had with coaster brakes or the new rear-wheel disc in 1972. The disc brake was only available when buying a five-speed model, and the 5-speed Krates now sold for $113.95. The original Krate lineup was discontinued in 1973.

The automotive style brake disc was squeezed by this cable-activated brake caliper.

This 1972 Orange Krate was fully equipped with a five-speed shifter and the new disc brake.

The World Voyageur was one of the first "Schwinn Approved" bikes that were imported from Japan. They were designed in Schwinn's American facilities but the construction was done overseas.

Barnard's Schwinn

Since the World Voyageur had no chain guard, the name was screen printed onto the diagonal frame tube.

By utilizing the derailleur and front sprockets, you could easily choose any of the ten speeds at your avail.

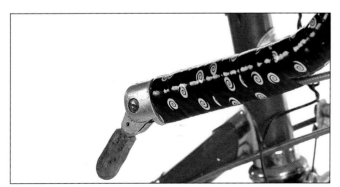

To select one of the 10 speeds on duty, all the rider needed to do was to manipulate one of the bar-end shift levers.

The front wheel was easily removed for transport via quick-release levers.

The girls weren't left out of the Sting-Ray mania: the Stardust was aimed directly at the sometimes skirt-wearing crowd.

Above: *Script was selected as the typeface for the Stardust moniker printed on the chain guard.*

Right: *Full-size handlebars were used on the Stardust along with hand levers for the brakes and a thumb-activated shift control.*

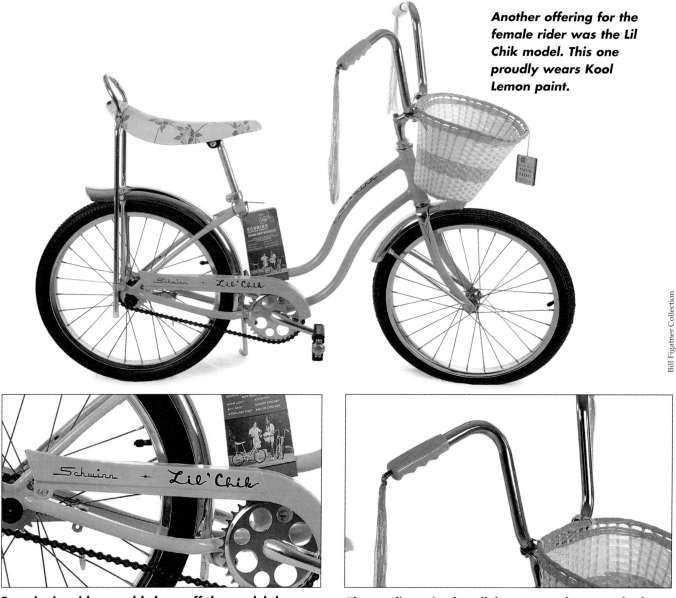

Another offering for the female rider was the Lil Chik model. This one proudly wears Kool Lemon paint.

Bill Figatner Collection

Even junior riders could show off the model they were riding as designated by the painted chain guard.

The medium-rise handlebars gave the same look as the full-sized Sting-Rays but provided an easier reach.

Lady riders got a new Varsity Sport also. Delivered with no fenders from the factory, they could be added for an extra fee. Models were offered in 19-inch (169) and 21-inch (171) frames and were sold in Sierra Brown, Campus Green, Orange and Lemon for $92.95

Along with expanding sales came trouble. By May of 1971, Schwinn had already sold out their production capacity for the year. Many dealers and customers would go without badly-wanted bikes unless additional capacity was created.

To meet this demand, Schwinn built a 100,000 square foot facility in Chicago. This $2.5 million plant opened in the early part of 1972. Plant 4 was able to build 1.5 million bikes per year. Even with the new plant in sight, Schwinn sold out of bikes in February of 1972. Previous to their painful loss of production capability, Schwinn had nearly always

The floral print saddle made no bones about the Lil Chik's target market.

The woven plastic basket was available in a variety of sizes and colors to match the bicycle's color scheme.

claimed a 30% share of the bicycle market. Being unable to fill the needs of many buyers cost the company a huge amount of that number. Falling to a low of nearly 12%, Schwinn desperately needed to get things back in gear.

Nineteen-seventy-two listings would still see the Krate bikes, as well as the bigger Manta-Rays, but a deceleration device was all the rage. Both five-speed versions of these models were now delivered with a disc brake on the rear wheel. The front brake on the Krates remained the drum used since day one, and the Manta-Ray squeezed the wheel with a caliper brake. Both bikes were also sold as coaster brake models too.

Nineteen seventy-two was the final year for the Manta-Ray. The coaster brake model sold for $69.95 while the five-speed went for $101.95. Colors available were Kool Orange, Kool Lemon or Campus Green. The Krates in their coaster brake trim sold for $82.95 while the five-speed went for $113.95. Only four model choices remained: Orange Krate, Lemon Peeler, Apple Krate and the Pea Picker.

In their effort to wean the younger riders off the soon-to-be-removed Krate models, Schwinn offered a 24-inch Varsity Sport. The trimmed-down variant was not lacking in features, and claimed caliper brakes at both ends and a ten-speed derailleur with Twin-Stik levers. The Varsity Sport was offered in Kool Lemon, Campus Green or Sierra Brown, and sold for $89.95 in 1972.

In that year, an effort to regain market share was made by importing their first bicycles from overseas. Designed and built to Schwinn's own exacting standards, the World Traveler and World Voyageur were offered in 21-inch and 23-inch frame sizes, as well as men's and women's styles. The ladies enjoyed an additional 19-inch frame option. Fewer than 2000 of these bikes came over in the first batch, but plans to ship in 200,000 more were in the works.

The Krate series, including the Apple Krate, was discontinued in 1973. The disc brake model was the most desired in the catalog.

Michael Mitchell

Left: *Disc brakes were offered on the 1972 and 1973 Krates and 1972 Manta Ray models and have become coveted items in the collector world.* **Middle:** *Both the five-speed and coaster brake Krates had the same printing on their chain guard. There was no distinction between the two screen-printed onto the side.* **Right:** *Both the headlight and taillight were generator driven and provided a fair amount of light as long as you were pedaling.*

The 1973 Sports Tourer was only one step below the world-class Paramount and delivered many of the same features at a lower sticker price.

Barnard's Schwinn

As with most of Schwinn's lightweight models, a lack of chain guard forced the position of the bicycle's name onto one of the frame tubes.

Nineteen seventy-three would prove to be a pivotal year at Schwinn. The Krate series had first appeared in 1968 and was an overnight sensation, helping Schwinn to sell a million bikes in a single year for the first time ever. As with any new trend, things start to cool down after a few years, and the Krate series was no different. Slowing sales resulted in the existence of only three versions for 1973. The

The ten speeds of the Sports Tourer were selected using the Twin-Stik shift levers mounted at the steering head of the frame.

Both the front and rear brakes were of the center-pull variety, which delivered an equal amount of pressure to each side of the wheel when speed needed to be reduced.

The shift levers told the sprockets and derailleur which gear to select upon the demand of the rider.

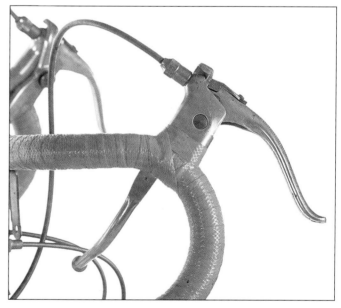

For the rider's convenience and safety, dual brake levers were on board the Sports Tourer. No matter the rider's posture, a brake lever was within easy reach.

Orange Krate, Apple Krate and Lemon Peeler were the sole survivors. Gone was the Pea Picker.

The paint applied to the 1973 Orange Krate was changed from Kool Orange to Sunset Orange. The seat covering and handgrips also changed accordingly. The coaster brake models were also removed from the catalog, and the five-speed models needed $119.95 to take them home.

In addition to lagging sales, Schwinn felt the influence of the government's concern over the safety of frame-mounted shift levers. Viewed as a threat, they would have to be removed from the

This gold edition Varsity was won by Jack Huvelhorst for correctly guessing how many pieces were used to assemble a Schwinn Varsity.

Bicycle Museum of America

1974 models.

Obviously a Krate bike without the Stik Shift just wasn't the same, so Schwinn decided to kill the line before the 1974 catalogs were printed. Sting-Rays survived the order to change the bars to a narrower dimension, but a Krate without a shifter was another story.

The top-of-the-line Paramount had first appeared in 1938, and until 1973 had never been offered with a lady's frame. The Deluxe Touring Paramount (P60) allowed women to enjoy the light weight and precise handling that the Paramount was known for. The Deluxe Touring Paramount provided the rider with fifteen speeds, while the Deluxe Paramount (P65) supplied only ten. Two frame sizes (20-inch and 22-inch) permitted the perfect fit that Schwinn was so adamant about. The choice of colors was anything in the Schwinn

It was a sad day in 1974 when the frame mounted Stik Shifts were ruled too dangerous by the government and removed from all bicycles in the U.S.

Another "fantasy" Krate model that never made the sales catalogs was the Koal Krate. Perhaps the poor sales of the all white Cotton Picker helped to kill the all-black Koal Krate before it had a chance to be introduced.

Andy and Wendy McGann Collection

catalog as well as black, white and Silver Mist. The price of this new model was not light, though, stated as $450.00 in the catalog.

For the boys that couldn't quite reach the pedals of a full-sized Varsity, the new Varsity Sport was introduced. The latest 24-inch frame still carried the full range of Varsity components, including the ten-speed gearing. Even the handlebars were made narrower to better fit a smaller rider. Weighing 36 pounds and offered in Kool Lemon, Campus Green

or Sunset Orange, the Varsity Sport sold for $102.95.

Another new version of indoor riding was also seen in the ergoMETRIC Exerciser. More accurate electronic calculations were now available while pedaling in place. This highly advanced version of the Exerciser sold for $450.00 while the base model was only $96.95.

Despite the loss of the beloved Krate bikes, several new entrants and feature upgrades were introduced in the 1974 catalog.

The mostly black theme was certainly stealthy, but maybe it was the bright colors that made the Krates such a success.

Imported bicycles had been a threat and a nuisance to Schwinn's offerings for many years, but the company still refused to sell a machine that was assembled overseas. Schwinn bikes were not without their share of imported accessories and components, but the actual units were always made in the USA. 1972 would show the world that you could teach an old manufacturer new tricks. Their earlier loss of market share due to a lack of capacity was addressed in part by bringing bikes in from overseas, despite their previous disdain for the idea. The World Traveler and World Voyageur were the first imports sold by Schwinn in the first few years of the 1970s.

The "Schwinn Approved" Le Tour was brought in for 1974 and was the third bike Schwinn imported for sale in the U.S.. Built in Japan, the Le Tour was a high quality piece that offered a lot of bike at a moderate price. The Le Tour could be purchased in one of three frame sizes: 21-inch (LT-1), 23-inch (LT-3) or 25-inch (LT-5). Regardless of the frame size you chose, they were well constructed

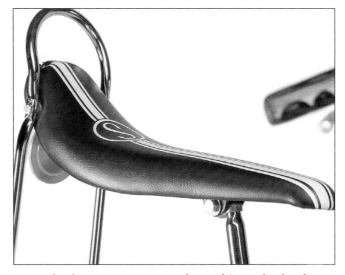

Even the banana seat was draped in a cloak of black, with only a racing stripe to brighten the gloom.

using the fully lugged and brazed process. Even the 27x1-1/4-inch Puff Gumwall tires were "Schwinn Approved." The spoked wheels could be easily removed with the quick-release aluminum alloy hubs. With a weight of only 30 to 32 pounds, depending on frame size and kickstand choice, the Le Tour was surely a lightweight model. All of the Le Tours carried ten-speeds and were sold in Opaque Blue, Opaque Red and Kool Lemon.

Although never a production model, the Grape Krate was considered as another offering in the Krate lineup in 1968.

Dipped in purple paint, the Grape Krate would have been an interesting option for Krate buyers at the time.

In keeping with the Krate family, the front wheel would have worn the same chrome fender up front as long as it was sold after the 1968 model year.

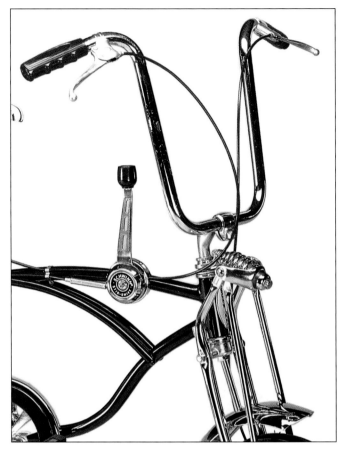

Standard issue Krate handlebars and frame-mounted shifter were to be part of the package.

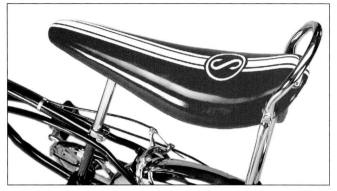

A vividly colored seat, complete with racing stripe was also in the Krate tradition.

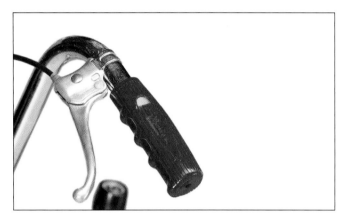

Grips that matched the vinyl seat covering played right into the theme.

The Sprint was another new model first seen in 1974. The Sprint was built around a shorter wheelbase which provided a "fun feel" to the ride. The carbon steel frame was sold in 22-inch (422) and 24-inch (424) varieties. The Twin-Stik gear selector allowed 10 different speeds, and the "Schwinn Approved" 38:100 derailleur handled the shifting duty. The Sprint weighed in at 36 to 37 pounds, again depending on the frame size chosen by the buyer. Opaque Blue, Opaque Red and Kool Lemon were also the available hues.

The ladies had a new choice in two-wheeled fun in 1974 in the Continental. The Continental had been around for many years, but never in a ladies' frame. The new version of the well-built Continental was also available in two frame sizes to

Naturally the seat would be provided with a pair of Krate shocks to finish off the project.

The "Schwinn-Approved" machine was the Le Tour of 1974. Built in Japan and imported into the USA, this bike would mark a change in the way Schwinn did business.

Brakes at both ends of the Le Tour were of the center-pull variety, and were cast in a featherweight alloy.

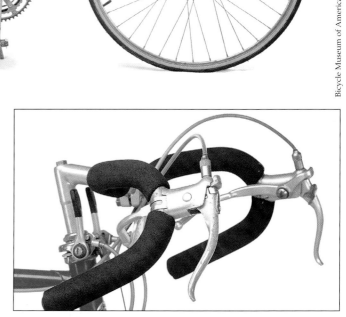

The racing nature of the lightweight LeTour was evident by the crouched riding position the rider assumed when grabbing the padded bars.

best fit the rider's needs. A 19-inch (369) and 21-inch (371) were both made from the same carbon steel used on other Schwinn lightweight models. A ten-speed, 38 to 100 derailleur gear was operated with the now standard Twin-Stik controls.

Center-pull caliper brakes slowed the ladies Continental, and 27x 1-1/4-inch High Performance Sports Touring tires met the road. Again weighing 36 to 37 pounds, depending on frame size, the ladies could have their choice of Opaque Blue, Kool Lemon or Chestnut in the paint department.

Also in the ladies' department, the Suburban models returned. With your choice of five or ten-

Quick release wheel hubs allowed the rider to swap fresh rubber more quickly.

27x 1-1/4-inch Puff Gumwall tires were standard equipment on the Le Tours.

The Le Tour was pitched as an "exceptional buy in lightweight ten-speed bikes" and weighed in at between 30 and 32 pounds, depending on the frame size and kickstand.

speeds and three different frame sizes, the Suburban offered a lot of flexibility. The ten-speed Suburbans carried a 38:100 gear, and were sold in 17-inch (667), 19-inch (669) and 21-inch (671) dimensions. The five-speed models were shown in 17-inch (567), 19-inch (569) and 21-inch (571) sizes, all with a 39:89 gear ratio.

New for the 1974 five-speed models was the application of the GT 120 derailleur and handlebar mounted shift control. This ratchet-type lever offered a new level of convenience to the lady rider. The same Deluxe mattress saddle, enameled fenders with contrasting color stripe and upright riding position remained in place. Opaque Blue, Lime and Chestnut were the color selections.

Two new 24-inch variants were also shown for the first time in the 1974 catalog. The 24-inch wheeled Breeze was a reduced dimension version

The Suburban made its debut in 1970 and was originally sold with your choice of three, five or 10 speeds. The 1974s were 10- or five-speed models, as seen here.

Barnard's Schwinn

Typically, the bike name would be screen-printed on the chain guard, but the Suburban had a simple decoration in its place.

For the five-speed variants, the GT-120 derailleur and ratchet-type shifter were new. A simple flick of the thumb allowed the rider to select any one of the five gears on tap.

Instead of the chain guard, the "Suburban" moniker was placed on the diagonal frame tube.

of the adult Breeze. The Breeze was built for the lady riders, and the 24-inch version catered to the younger crowd.

The Speedster was the boys' equivalent of the Breeze and also sported 24-inch wheels. The camelback frame was crafted of carbon steel and carried the rider on a cushioned saddle. Both the smaller Breeze and Speedster wore chrome fenders front and rear, and came in Kool Lemon, Opaque

The Junior Sting-Ray allowed smaller riders to keep up with the bigger kids yet still have a Sting-Ray.

The "Sting-Ray" script was far more obvious than the "Junior" screen print, thus allowing a certain degree of respect for the smaller rider.

Blue and Opaque Red iterations.

The Sting-Ray Fastback was still included amongst the youth group of bikes, but now carried the GT 120 derailleur and handlebar-mounted shift control. Kool Lemon and Sunset Orange were the only color choices available.

A pair of low-rise bars kept the grips within easy reach.

Schwinn

Motocross and Mountain Bikes

Chapter 9

The body of the deceased Krate series was not even cold before America's youth began to embrace a new form of bicycle fun. BMX, or Bicycle Moto Cross, was sweeping the nation, and it didn't take Schwinn long to detect and pick up on the trend. Before too long the Schwinn catalog held a wide variety of BMX bikes for the eager young riders. The acceptance of imported "Schwinn Approved" models also caused a swelling of the ranks as the company realized the benefits of selling the high-quality bikes that cost far less to manufacture.

No longer touting claims of high fashion and glamour, the ladies' Hollywood still carried itself well in 1975.

Blue Moon Bikes Ltd.

The 1975 cast of characters had a few new players in both the new BMX class as well as the lightweight division.

The LeTour was "Schwinn Approved" and first seen in 1974. For 1975 the LeTour with a Mixte frame was sold as well. The top tube of this frame design was angled downward, and poised for use by the female riders. Lugged steel was the primary component used in assembly. Ten speeds were on board as were center pull caliper brakes, complete with two position brake levers. Araya steel tubular rims were on duty to keep the 27x1-1/4-inch Puffwall tires in their place. Two frame sizes were offered, and both the 19-inch (L-69) and 22-inch (L-72) left the LeTour with a weight of about 32 pounds. Yellow was offered alongside Opaque Red and Opaque Blue.

The Schwinn Approved World Voyageur returned to the catalog in 1975, but was now known as the Voyageur II. The Voyageur II was second in line to the Paramount, and offered many of the same traits with a lower cost of ownership. The frame was constructed of 4130 chrome-moly alloy tubing and double butted for strength.

Araya aluminum alloy rims held 27x 1-1/4-inch LeTour tires in place. Braking was delivered by a pair of center-pull calipers, controlled by dual position, handlebar mounted levers. Three frame sizes were listed: 21-inch (V21), 23-inch (V23) and 25-inch (V25). The Voyageur II weighed 27-28 pounds which was only 4 or 5 pounds more than the featherweight Paramount. Silver and Opaque red were the color options in 1975.

The next import model Schwinn brought in for 1975 was the Traveler. Gone was the "World" moniker, but a ladies' model helped to fill the void. Both the men's and women's versions were built using the brazed lug frame technique.

This method provided adequate strength at a lower cost to manufacture, which resulted in a less expensive bicycle. Ten-twenty (1020) carbon steel was used in place of the more costly 4130 alloy steel used on the Paramount and Voyageur II. The ladies' model featured the downward sloping top frame tube that allowed for more "ladylike" entrance and exit. Ten speeds were on tap on both models as well. Side-pull caliper brakes mounted on fore and aft tires did the slowing. Dual position brake levers provided some flexibility to the rider's chosen position. The men's frame was sold in 21-inch (W21) and 23-inch (W23) sizes but the ladies' model was one size only at 19-inch (W69). Araya steel tubular rims replaced the more costly alloy versions, and Puff gumwall tires replaced the LeTours found elsewhere. Either sex had the choice of Opaque Red or Opaque Blue for their Traveler. A weight of 32 pounds was all the Traveler could claim.

Aimed directly at female riders of lesser stature, the Collegiate Sport model came in smaller frame sizes and rolled on reduced dimension tires and wheels. The standard drop handlebars and dual position brake levers made the smaller rider feel right at home with the bigger boys and girls.

A Single-Stik shift lever controlled the five speeds of the Sport model. 26x1-3/8-inch gumwall tires were mated with tubular rims. Both the 17-inch (787) and 19-inch (789) were sold with no fenders, but they could be added as an extra cost option. Depending on the frame size chosen, the Collegiate Sport weighed between 39 and 41 pounds and was painted in your choice of Flamboyant Red, Lime Green or Yellow.

For those who were eager yet not tall enough for the full-sized lightweights, Schwinn introduced four new 24-inch tire models in 1975. Both a girls' and boys' version of the Varsity Sport were shown with the new 24-inch tire. Both versions shifted through 10 speeds with the Twin-Stik gear levers. Side-pull calipers activated the dual-position brake levers. The frames were reduced slightly from the full-sized Varsity but carbon steel was still used to construct them. The drop handlebars were also narrower than on the standard Varsity models to provide a comfortable reach for the smaller rider. The boys' model (144) and the girls' (194) both came stock without fenders, but such could be added for an additional fee. Whether adorned with chrome fenders or not, Chestnut, Lime Green and Yellow were the optional colors for both varieties.

The Speedster delivered a compact package for the smaller male rider. The camelback frame was made of steel, and the upright "tourist style" bars and cushioned saddle made for a hospitable ride. The Speedster could be purchased with five speeds (K30-9) or in a coaster brake model (K30-6). The five-speed version slowed with a pair of caliper brakes. A pair of chrome fenders accented the Flamboyant Red or Sky Blue paint.

The Breeze offered the same equipment found on the Speedster, but was fashioned for the female rider. It was also sold in either a five-speed (K80-9) or coaster brake (K80-6) model. The same color options were also available on the Breeze that the Speedster offered.

Down the hall from the lightweight models came the BMX variants. Although still in its infancy, the BMX craze was seen as the next big wave in the bicycle world.

The Scrambler would open the door to many

The screen-printed chain guard was the only marquee announcing the Hollywood to the crowds.

variations on a theme and provided a basic mount for the BMX rider. Built around a 20-inch Sting-Ray chassis, the Scrambler (BX1-6) was assembled with reinforced welds for added strength. A forged front fork also provided an extra measure of durability for off-road terrain. A hardened steel crank and a braced handlebar also delivered more strength to the model. The studded tread design of the MX tires allowed for traction under the worst conditions, and the padded MX saddle gave the rider a decent perch for the few moments of seat time he might encounter. The Scrambler weighed a sturdy 38 pounds and could be purchased in Metallic Silver Mist, Sunset Orange or Metallic Gold.

For those riders who coveted a Scrambler but whose feet wouldn't reach the ground, the Mini-Scrambler (J49-6) was also rolled out in 1975. The smaller frame was fitted with 16-inch tires at both ends. A Gripper Slik was found out back and was covered by a flat black fender. The front tire was ribbed, and went without a fender. The braced handlebars were finished in flat black too, as was the MX saddle. Silver Mist or Sunset orange were the choices a rider faced when buying his new Mini Scrambler.

Since riders of all ages and sizes were getting in on the BMX fun, a Super Pixie (J46-6) was introduced in 1975 to fit the more diminutive MX buyer.

Sixteen-inch tires and wheels kept the Super Pixie close to earth. The Sunset Orange paint was offset by the dull black finish of the front and rear fenders. The braced handlebar and Scrambler style MX saddle were also trimmed in black. The Super Pixie was also a convertible model, allowing the top frame tube to be removed for use by boys or girls.

In the latter part of the 1970's, Schwinn seemed to roll out new models faster than ever seen before.

The continuing lightweight market growth was fed by numerous new entries, and the gas crunch was bringing all sorts of new riders into the showrooms. The BMX fad was on a continuing upswing, and new models addressed that need, too.

Nineteen seventy-six saw America's bicentennial, and Schwinn offered many models in celebratory paint. Single, three and five-speed Sting-Rays were available in Red, Blue, or a Red, White and Blue scheme. Single and three-speed Fair Lady models could also be done in the Red, White and Blue paint. All Varieties of the Varsity, including men's and women's 24-inch and 26-inch frame models were also sold in white with plenty of red and blue trim to carry off the theme.

Near the top of the food chain was the all-new "Schwinn Approved" Volare for 1977. It was one of the new Super Lite machines that Schwinn was selling and it rated near the Paramount. Designed by Schwinn engineers and lovingly assembled in Japan, the Volare had a frame constructed from Reynolds 531 double-butted tubing. This lightweight material allowed the Volare to weigh only 2 pounds more than the Paramount, which was an industry standard at only 23 pounds.

The Volare offered the rider a choice of 10 speeds selectable via the frame-mounted shift levers. Dura-Ace quick release hubs were found at both ends, and Araya 700x28C rims kept the Super 700C high pressure tires and tubes on duty.

Rat-trap pedals were complete with toe clips, straps and reflectors. Dura-Ace side pull brakes helped bring the Volare down from speed. A seamless racing saddle was constructed using a nylon base. As in almost all Schwinn bikes, a variety of frame sizes was listed. The catalog listed a 21-inch (VL-1), 23-inch (VL-3) and 25-inch (VL-5) for the Volare in 1977. Scarlet or Pearlescent Orange were the frame finish options, and $495 put one in your hands.

The "Schwinn Approved" Traveler was another member of the Super Lite club for 1977. The Traveler supplied the rider with ten-speed performance at a lower ticket price. The diamond design frame was crafted from 1020 carbon steel and was connected with brazed lug construction with single butted top and down tubes. Araya steel rims were wrapped with 27x 1-1/4-inch Puff gumwall tires. Dual position brake levers activated the side pull alloy calipers and shifting was done with convenient handlebar mounted levers. Rat-trap pedals came with reflectors only. The three frame sizes, 21-inch (T21), 23-inch (T23) and 25-inch (T25), were available in Flamboyant red or Sky Blue finishes. The Traveler weighed 32 pounds and retailed for $142.95.

A hot new model for 1977 was the Caliente. Both

The saddle provided all the comfort a Hollywood diva could ask for.

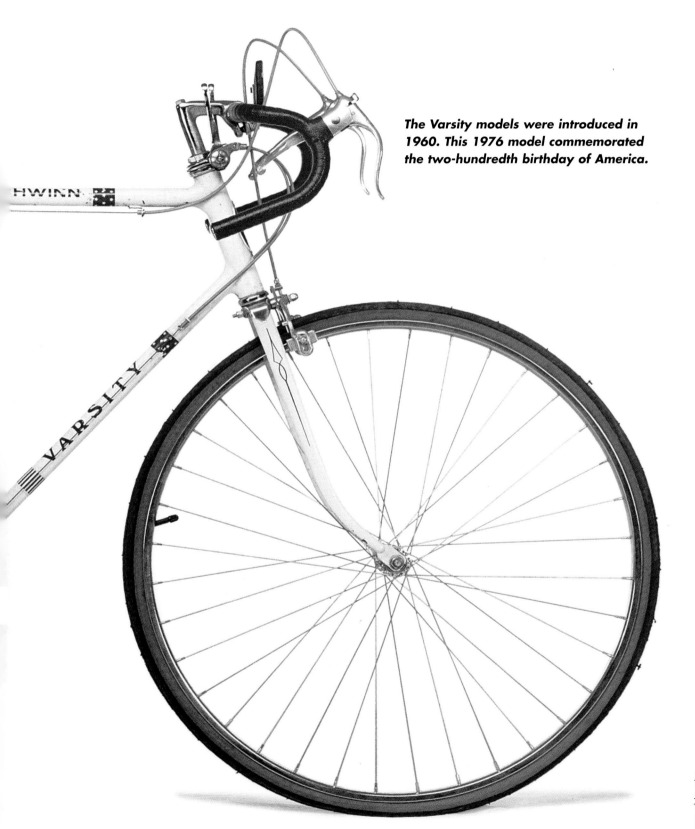

The Varsity models were introduced in 1960. This 1976 model commemorated the two-hundredth birthday of America.

men's and women's models were offered and incorporated several new bits of technology. Frame construction on the Caliente was "Schwinn built one piece electro-forged." More technology was found in the gear shifting department. Positron PPS, or Positive Pre-Select, was applied to the rear derailleur for swift and certain gear changes. The front sprocket was now fitted with the FF System, or free wheeling front sprocket. This allowed the Caliente to be shifted without being in motion. Great for selecting a lower gear for takeoffs without having to start out in a super high gear.

Chrome plating was applied to the 27-inch rims, drop style handlebars, forged stem and crank. "Schwinn Approved" (imported) side pull calipers were mounted for use on both wheels. Rat-trap pedals with reflectors provided positive grip for the rider's feet.

Both versions were sold in several frame sizes and colors. For the men, 20-inch (C20), 22-inch (C22), and 24-inch (C24) were listed with Sky Blue and Lime Green the available hues.

The ladies choices were limited to a 17-inch (C67) or 20-inch (C70) frame and the same colors as the men. The 1977 Caliente sold for $149.95, regardless of frame size or color.

With the fuel crisis in full bloom, Schwinn offered the Metro-Cycle as a way to beat the long lines and high prices at the pump. Sold in both men's and women's frame styles, it provided plenty of functionality as well as a comfortable way to get to your destination. Frames were once again the electro-forged one-piece diamond design with tubular front forks. Painted, full-coverage fenders kept the rider dry, and 28x1-3/8-inch Breeze

gumwalls mounted to chrome-plated tubular rims rolled within. Three speeds were on tap and could be selected with the handlebar mounted click shift control. Braking was delivered via coaster brake. The black mattress saddle allowed for longer rides than the racing style pillions. A pair of wire baskets hung off the rear spring carrier to provide storage space for those riding with baggage or groceries. The generator-driven head and taillights let riders get to and from their destinations even after the sun had set.

Men's frame sizes included 20-inch (M20-8), 22-inch (M22-8), and 24-inch (M24-8). The ladies had 17-inch (M67-8) and 22-inch (M72-8) to choose from. Any color you wanted was offered as long as it was Chestnut. As the ads put it, the Metro-Cycles sold for $139.95, "the price of about ten tanks of gas."

The BMX race continued to be strong, and several new models were shown in 1977's catalog. The MAG Scrambler was another variation on the previous Scrambler floor plan. Construction was identical to the Scrambler, but a pair of 20-inch nylon, fiberglass-reinforced wheels replaced the spoked rims.

The 1977 MAG Scrambler was peddled in several colors. Flamboyant Red, Sky Blue, or chrome were offered on the complete bike. A complete MAG model (BX6-8) would set you back $144.95 in Red or Blue, and an additional $10 got you the all-chrome version (BX9-6). For those wanting to create their own racing machine, the frame was available as a separate purchase. When buying the frame alone, you had more color choices at your fingertips: Flamboyant Red, Sky Blue, Black, Green, Silver Mist and the all chrome version. The

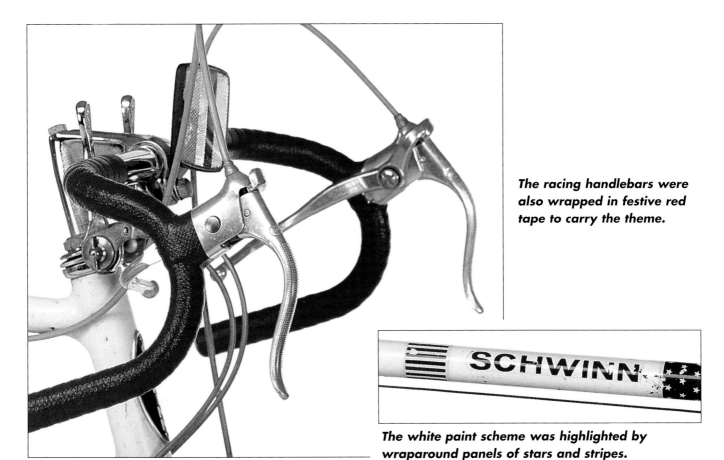

The racing handlebars were also wrapped in festive red tape to carry the theme.

The white paint scheme was highlighted by wraparound panels of stars and stripes.

painted choices (FX1-0) sold for $39.95 and the chrome variant (FX2-0) was $49.95.

Another choice for the BMX rider was the Scrambler 36/36. The frame design was less substantial than the others, but still delivered plenty of rugged performance. The 36/36 rode on spoked wheels and 20-inch studded tires. The 36/36 weighed one more pound than the MAG version. Paint choices for the $119.95 36/36 (BX6-6) were Flamboyant Red and Sky Blue. The all chrome edition (BX7-6) sold for 10 dollars more.

If you were willing to forgo some durability and weight, and preferred more style in your BMX mount, the Hornet and Tornado may have been up your alley. Both built around the Sting-Ray cantilever frame, these models were fitted with several components that set them apart from the other models. The Hornet had a three-dimensional molded tank to mimic a real MX motorcycle mounted to its upper cross member.

Painted fenders on both wheels and a matching chain guard added to the visual appeal. The number plate attached to the braced handlebars showed you were serious. The over-stuffed MX saddle provided lots of comfort for the days you weren't attacking the craggy terrain. The Hornet (J33-6) sold for $116.95 in either Black with Yellow and Orange trim, or Yellow with Black and Orange trim.

A less decorated variant was the Tornado. Still doing a great job at posing as a real MX machine, the Tornado's "tank" was nothing more than a flat piece of molded plastic that filled the space in the cantilever frame. The saddle was not as thoroughly

The Hornet brought a real touch of "motorcycle" to the bike owner with its long list of grownup features.

padded, but the painted fenders and chain guard were still in place. Maybe not as realistic as the Hornet, at least the selling price was. Selling for $84.95, the J32-6 had a black frame with Yellow and Orange trim, or an Orange frame with Black and Yellow trim.

The final BMX model in the 1977 catalog was the Hurricane 5. As the name suggests, this model came with a five-speed derailleur and a handlebar Positron II Stik-Shift gear changer mounted between the handlebars. Side-pull caliper brakes were found on both 20-inch wheels, with control levers also mounted on the handlebars. A fully padded MX saddle, BMX grips and cross-braced bars were all part of the Hurricane 5. The J34-9 featured a Silver Mist frame with either blue and white or red and white trim and sold for $136.95.

Outside the lightweight and BMX realm, a few other models joined the ranks in 1977. The Spitfire (CC7-6) was a heavy-duty bike complete with 26x2-1/8-inch balloon tires and rims. Knobby whitewall tires let the rider go on or off-road with equal aplomb.

The molded fuel tank was done in three-dimensions, just like the real thing, but held no liquid.

From the factory the Spitfire rode with open wheels, but a pair of chrome fenders could be purchased for some protection in wet weather. The cantilever frame was electro-forged. Even the black saddle was heavy duty and well padded. The Spitfire was offered only in a single-speed, coaster brake style. Flamboyant Red, Sky Blue and Black versions all sold for $116.95.

The 20-inch wheel Typhoon (L32-6) was shown in the 1977 catalog as well, and was aimed at the 5-to-7-year-old boys. The electro-forged cantilever frame was sturdy and sported a pair of chrome fenders. A coaster brake was on duty to do the stopping. Sky Blue and Flamboyant Red were again the color choices. The Typhoon sold for $77.95.

The Schwinn Sting-Ray had already earned its status as an icon, but remained in the 1977 lineup due to remaining demand. The latest version of venerable Sting-Ray featured three speeds (J38-8) and a coaster brake. The catalog also listed a coaster brake model (J38-6) and a five-speed (J38-9). The five-speed model stopped with a pair of side pull caliper brakes. The coaster brake model weighed 37-1/2 pounds while the five-speed version was listed at 41 pounds. Prices for the 1977 models were as follows: Coaster, $89.95; three-speed Coaster, $109.95; and five-speed Coaster, $122.95. All versions were available in Flamboyant Red, Sky Blue or Sunset Orange.

The 1978 edition had no fewer than ten different BMX style machines. Most were returning models from the previous years.

For those riders who took their BMX activity more seriously, there was the Scrambler Competition SX1000, model BX2-6. This example

The full-length BMX saddle gave the appearance of a real cycle and provided the rider with extra comfort.

was built around a chrome-moly frame with reinforced gussets. The chrome-moly front fork held an alloy, tubular rim and a 20x2-1/8-inch Scrambler tire.

The rear rim was also alloy, measured 20x2-inch, and was shod with a Schwinn Skin Competition Tire. The alloy frame and wheels added up to only 28 pounds, giving the competitive rider the edge over heavier machines. Color choices for the BX2-6 were Silver Mist with Red trim or Chestnut with Yellow trim. Either choice carried a retail price of $184.95.

If more flash was desired the SX1000 was also offered in an all-chrome version, and Model #BX3-6 sold for $194.95.

A less serious rider could opt for the SX100 model B10-6. This style carried a steel frame but saved weight by using fiberglass mag wheels instead of the spoke type. A pair of 20x2-1/8-inch studded tires completed the package. Available in

Silver Mist with Red trim, or Chestnut with Yellow trim, it sold for $166.95.

Also available were frames only in Flamboyant Red, Sky Blue, Silver Mist, Black and Green variants. The-all chrome option (FX2-0) went for $52.95.

The Sting-Ray BX combined many styling highlights of the classic bike with additions better suited to the off-road rider. Chrome plated rims and fenders mated to BMX knobby tires provided a nice mix of old and new. The Sting-Ray BX, Model J37-6, retailed at $99.95, and was sold in either Flamboyant Red or Sky Blue.

For the smaller rider, Schwinn offered the Sting-Ray BX Mini-Scrambler. The 16-inch wheels and tires kept the smaller rider close to the ground, but offered plenty of fun. The black Sting-Ray saddle was offset by the Silver Mist or Flamboyant red frame. The J49-6 sold for $89.95.

Two entire pages of the 1978 catalog were

devoted to additional BMX accessories for your Schwinn bike. Whether you were a beginner or serious competitor, options were available to suit every need.

Along with the raft of BMX bikes, Schwinn still sold a wide variety of machines for all types of riders. The X-tra Lite models were a popular choice for those seeking a well-built yet lightweight model. Many of the "Schwinn Approved" import models fell under this category in 1978.

The Volare, Super Le Tour 12.2, Le Tour III and Traveler III were all listed in the sales materials. Ranging in price from the Traveler III at $157.95 to the Volare at $579.95, there was a model that fit both your size requirement and budget.

For those who still preferred to do their riding indoors, the Air-dyne stationary bike was also introduced in 1978. For the truly well-balanced rider, the Giraffe Unicycle was also rolled out in 1978. With a saddle that towered six feet from the pavement, it took practice and skill to get up and keep moving. The entry fee for this circus act was $109.95 and all-chrome was the only color offered.

Along with a catalog that was filled with a wide variety of machines, more than 6,000 accessories were offered to provide the rider with any

The rear seat supports did double duty as faux shock absorbers, complete with the accordion "gators."

The braced handlebars were complete with a roll of safety padding and a number plate.

imaginable option for his or her bike.

The year 1979 would see the addition of several new models, but none would reinvent the wheel, so to speak.

Weighing in at 28 pounds and shifting through 12 speeds, the new Super Le Tour II was all new and part of the growing X-tra Lite category. Still built in the Chicago plant, the Super Le Tour II featured a brazed lug frame, and downtube mounted shift levers. Shimano provided the required drive train components while Weinmann delivered the 27x1-1/4-inch alloy rims and side pull brakes complete with alloy levers. Your choice of 21-inch (D21-9), 23-inch (D23-9) or 25-inch (D25-9) frames

were available in Black Sable, Frosty Blue or Strawberry Red paint. A retail price of $249.95 was listed in the Zone 1 catalog.

Down the road a piece was the "Schwinn Approved" World Sport, which delivered ten-speed performance at a bargain basement price. For only $139.95 (Zone 1) you had a choice in both men's and women's frames, as well as Pearl Blue or Royal Maroon finishes. Men's sizes were 21-inch (W11-9), 23-inch (W13-9) and 25-inch (W15-9). Women had their pick of 19-inch (W69-9) or 21-inch (W71-9) chassis. Suntour shift levers were handlebar stem mounted for ease of access. The World Sport weighed 33 pounds complete with kickstand.

The chain guard was reverse-screen printed with the Hornet name.

The Hurricane 5 gave the rider a great balance of comfort and pseudo-BMX qualities all wrapped up in one machine.

The Spitfire models were revamped in 1979. An electro-forged cantilever frame carried the 2.125-inch balloon tires, and there were several optional packages for wheel and gear packages. The Spitfire I coaster brake models were sold in 24-inch (CC1-6) or 26-inch (CC1-7) wheel sizes. The Spitfire V (CC5-5) traveled on 26-inch wheels and provided the rider a choice of five speeds. Whether in Cardinal Red, Sky Blue or Black Sable, the Spitfire I sold for $136.95 while the Spitfire V went for $169.95.

The BMX group was still expanding rapidly and a few new faces were seen in the catalog. The SX 500 sported a new flash-welded carbon steel frame and Magalloy alloy wheels. A competition saddle and

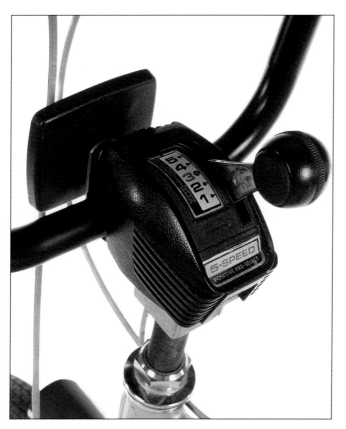

To get around the government ruling on frame mounted shifters, the Hurricane 5 had the mechanism attached to the steering head stem.

braced handlebars joined the fray.

The painted models (B11-6) were available in Silver Mist or Spicy Chestnut, and another all-chrome (B12-6) variant was also listed. Zone 1 prices ran $174.95 for the painted models and $184.95 for the chrome.

For the BMX rider on a budget, the Phantom Scrambler was the ticket in. The BMX frame, braced handlebars and competition saddle could be combined with spoke wheels or nylon Mags instead. The spoked wheel variants (B15-6) sold for $119.95 while the Mag wheel model (B16-6) cost another $30. The Mag wheel models were Black Sable with Red Wheels, Cardinal Red with Black wheels or Sky Blue with Black wheels. Listed weight was 33 pounds for both versions.

The Sting-Ray name was alive and well 16 years after its first appearance. The Mini-Sting-Ray let smaller riders take to the streets on their downsized machine. Sixteen-inch studded BMX tires and a cantilever frame provided strength and flexible riding options. The Mini was sold in Sky Blue or Cardinal Red, and both colors were accented by silver trim. The 32-pound Mini-Sting-Ray sold for $89.95.

Overall sales of Schwinn bikes reached a total approaching 1.3 million in 1979, and that was from a network of only 1700 dealers. In contrast, 1951 claimed over 5000 dealers and sales of only around 300,000 units. Although the sales picture in general appeared healthy enough in 1979, a large decline in the children's division had resulted in many of the smaller models being phased out. Once a child left his Sting-Ray or Krate, he or she seemed to gravitate to other brands and models. This lack of owner

A long padded saddle was supported with a pair of simulated shock absorbers.

loyalty was hurting Schwinn, and they knew a new approach was required to stanch the loss of customers. Even with this shrinking customer base, 900,000 bikes were sold by Schwinn in 1980.

Changes in the 1980 lineup went on unabated, and all segments of riders were addressed. An all-new "Schwinn Approved," Xtra Lite model was introduced as the Voyageur 11.8, 12 speed. Double-butted top and bottom frame tubes were formed from 4130 chrome-moly tubing, and the rear stays were chrome plated. A Shimano Altus LT derailleur was used along with quick-release wheels for added performance and convenience. Dia-Compe 500G side pull calipers supplied the stopping power to the 27x1-1/4-inch Araya alloy rims. Schwinn Super Record gumwall, high-pressure tires kept the rims off the road. Three frame sizes

were available in three color choices each. All three frames choices gave the buyer a choice of Scarlet Flame, Black Sable, or an all chrome option. Frame sizes of 21-inch (V21-9 painted, VC1-9 chrome), 23-inch (V23-9 painted, VC3-9 chrome) and 25-inch (V25-9 painted, VC5-9 chrome) were listed.

For those who sought "the excitement of true lightweight bicycling but need a thrifty price," the "Schwinn Approved" World Ten Speed was released in 1980 as well. Although not as light as the Paramount, at only 33 pounds the World model faired well in the division. It was sold in both men's and women's frame styles and provided a choice of two colors, Frosty Silver or Royal Maroon, as well as several chassis sizes. Men could ride a 21-inch (W31-9), 23-inch (W33-9) or 25-inch (W35-9) while women had a 19-inch (W89-9) or 21-inch (W91-9)

A psychedelic rendering of "Hurricane 5" was screened onto the chain guard.

decision to make. A racing saddle and drop style bars showed their racing intentions.

The World Tourist models featured mattress saddles and tourist style, upright bars mated to the running gear of the World. A pair of slender chrome fenders were also in place on the World Tourist where the World ran with none. The World Tourist was only sold in Sky Blue, but still offered the same frame size options as the World.

The BMX phenomenon was still running strong, and Schwinn introduced the SX-2000 to meet with increasing demand for new and more durable bikes.

Both the Sting (B25-0), first seen on tracks in 1979, and the SX-2000 (B22-0) were constructed of 4130 chrome-moly alloy tubing that was ovalized and double-butted for extreme strength while still staying light. The steering head tube was five inches in length to bring extra strength to one of a bike frame's most abused segments. Wheel rims on both models were anodized aluminum. Both of these models delivered the highest level of BMX performance that Schwinn could muster. The frames of each model were also sold in stand-alone form for those who desired to build a truly individual machine.

In the lightweight division, several new contenders entered the ring in 1981. The Superior was assembled using Campagnolo Gran Sport components, "Perfect for a good hard ride" in the words of the sales catalog of the time. Only sold in Pearl Orange, it was available in four different frame sizes: 19-inch (219), 21-inch (221), 23-inch

(223) and 25-inch (225) made choosing the correct size a breeze. A weight of only 24.8 pounds meant you could rack up some serious miles on your ride.

Pedals complete with toe clips and straps held your feet firmly in place while brazed-on water bottle fittings held your liquid refreshment. The Superior also carried a retail price of $850, regardless of frame size.

Joining the Le Tour family in 1981, the Tourist model offered light weight with a touring saddle and upright handlebars. Cushioned grips provided comfort to the rider's hands a well. A pair of chrome fenders added a touch of flash as well as keeping the rider dry. The added features did bump up the weight a bit to 29.3 pounds. Frame sizes for the men included 21-inch (D311), 23-inch (D331) and 25-inch (D351). Women's sizes were 19-inch (D791) and 22-inch (D821). Colors for either the men's or women's models were Spicy Chestnut or Sky Blue. All versions of the Le Tour Tourist sold for $254.95 in 1981.

Another new model for the grow-ups was the Sports Tourer. It was still sold within the X-tra Lite group, but was built with some heavier-duty components for added durability. The men could choose between 21-inch (9211), 23-inch (9231), 25-inch (9251), or for an added fee the 27-inch (9271) frame. Women's frames were 19-inch (9691) or 22-inch (9721) and all varieties sold for $229.95. You could have any color you wanted as long as it was Black Sable with red trim.

"A big new attraction" was shown in the 1981 catalog: the Sprint. Positioned as an economical new lightweight, the Sprint was presented in several frame sizes nonetheless. For the men, a 17-inch (S17), 20-inch (S20) and 22-inch (S22) were presented. Women had their choice of 17-inch (S57) or 20-inch (S60) frames. Only one color, Frosty Silver, was listed.

Opaque red handlebar tape and matching red badges completed the ensemble. Schwinn's "regular Electro-forged frame" was the basis for the latest entry, which was mated to other "regular" Schwinn components to keep the cost down. A retail price of only $166.95 was the proof of their efforts.

Along with the raft of BMX bikes, Schwinn still sold a wide variety of machines for all types of riders. The X-tra Lite models were a popular choice.

The BMX craze was still raging and Schwinn made several new additions to their tool box. Although the Scrambler had been first seen in 1978, the new versions were far more purpose-built. While the previous version was based on the Sting-Ray cantilever frame, the 1981 Scrambler (B431) models touted a double-gusseted structure that was all new. A rigid chrome-plated front fork could be added to blend with the standard chrome spoke wheels. Front and rear caliper brakes could also be added at the buyer's discretion. MAG wheels were

The Mini Sting-Ray was an updated version of the Junior model seen in previous years.

Matt Mutchler Collection

yet another extra-cost option.

The Scrambler MAG (411) sold for $196.95 while the standard Scrambler went for $181.95. Spicy Chestnut, Frosty Silver or Cardinal Red were the colors on tap.

Two lower-cost models were also made available in the Phantom (B461) and Phantom MAG (B451). Both bikes rode on the same frame as the Scramblers, but had fewer ups and extras to keep weight and cost down. The Phantom carried its studded tires on chrome-spoked wheels while the MAG edition wore tough nylon "mag" rims. Both styles were sold in your choice of Sky Blue with Yellow highlights or Black Sable with Yellow wheels and trim. The Phantom sold for $144.95 and the MAG went for $181.95.

The final new member of the 1981 gang was the Thrasher, model B511. Once again based on the Scrambler frame, it offered a no-frills approach to BMX racing. Studded tires were mated to spoked wheels, and a forged fork held it together. Chrome cross-braced handlebars were fitted with blue grips to match the chain guard. It was sold only in Frosty Silver and carried a price tag of $134.95.

When compared to other new model years, 1982 would be seen as a slow day in the newsroom. While there were improvements made on several models in each segment, only two fresh faces were seen.

Truth be told, the first "fresh" face was not new at all, but the Paramount was now being offered as a "custom tailored" machine. Over 1000 different configurations of frames and drive train components were available, basically guaranteeing the proper fit of the rider and his specific riding

In contrast to Schwinn's usual placement of the company and model names, the chain guard was devoid of either but was instead decorated with graphics.

needs. Only the finest in Reynolds 531 double-butted tubing was used to lovingly manufacture a Paramount, and no detail went unattended.

The Voyageur SP was an all-new model for Schwinn but was still based on previous entrants in the catalog. The Voyageur SP provided a combination of fifteen speeds along with comfort and convenience features not found on other lightweight models. High-grade 4130 chrome-moly tubing was used to create the frame, and a pair of carrier racks were mounted as an integral part of the construction. Slightly larger 27x1-1/4-inch tires delivered added comfort without sacrificing weight. At only 27 pounds, the Voyageur SP seemed the perfect combination. No women's frames were

shown, but the men had 19-inch (V391), 21-inch (V411), 23-inch (V431), 25-inch (V451) or 27-inch (V471) sizes to choose from. Black Sable or Silver Blue Metallic were the available tints.

Only 6 of the 64 pages in the 1982 catalog were devoted to bikes outside the lightweight, all-terrain and BMX categories, proving how dominant they had become in the world of Schwinn bicycles. This trend continued in 1983 as new models remained within the aforementioned groups.

The LeTour Luxe was the first new name shown in the catalog for that year. The Luxe was slotted in between the Super and the standard Le Tour, and offered the buyer a small step between the upper and lower end models. The entire frame was composed of 4130 chrome-moly tubing and the fork was Tange hi-tensile steel.

A Sugino DNJS-2S aero crankset allowed the rider to deliver the power to the Shimano Altus LT derailleur. Alloy rims held Super Record tires in place. Both the Le Tour and Le Tour Luxe were sold in men's and Mixte frames. Men had their choice of 19-inch, 21-inch, 23-inch, 25-inch-inch and 27-inch models while the Mixte chassis was available in 19-inch and 22-inch varieties. All the sizes listed had Dark Blue or Dark Grey as listed paint options. The Luxe edition weighed 27-1/2 pounds, which was only 1-1/2 pounds more than the high end Super Le Tour.

Many changes in the BMX family were cosmetic or based in the new Series listings of models. Within the Predator Team Series, the Team 24 was a new listing. More closely related to a cruiser model, the Team 24 rolled on 24-inch wheels and tires but featured many of the same advances as the BMX models. A lightweight chrome-moly frame was steered by a pair of custom designed handlebars. The Team 24 was slowed by a pair of Dia-Compe MX900 caliper brakes that grabbed Araya 7x rims. The Maximizer tires were a patented Schwinn design, endorsed by the factory BMX racing team. Finished in Show Chrome with Black trim, the Team 24 weighed in at 28.4 pounds.

In the adult all-terrain category, the Sierra model was first shown. Sold in 18-inch and 21-inch sizes, the Sierra featured frames made from flash-welded 1010 carbon steel and steered with a Tange, high-tensile steel fork. Twenty-six-inch by 1/-3/4-inch Ukai alloy rims were squeezed by Dia-Compe 860 alloy cantilever brakes with mountain levers.

The Schwinn designed mountain handlebars were 29-inch wide and rose 6 inches to meet the rider's hands. An Avocet Touring saddle made for a comfortable pillion. Midnight Blue and Chestnut were the listed colors for either frame size.

The Manta-Ray name was resurrected for 1983 and was applied to a bike that was seen in the BMX and Family section of the catalog. A double-gusseted, 1010 carbon steel fork was fronted by a tubular leading axle fork for durability and accurate steering. The rear hub held a coaster brake, and the 19-tooth sprocket was also of the Shimano brand. Union Rattrap pedals moved the 1/2x1/8-inch chain per the rider's demands. The 30 pound

The Sting-Ray name was emblazoned on the top frame tube instead of on the chain guard.

The side of the saddle was one place the Schwinn name was placed on the Mini-Sting-Ray for 1980.

Manta-Ray was sold only in Black paint with yellow graphics. The chrome handlebars were capped off with a pair of yellow grips.

The lightweight division saw two new entries for 1984, as did the mountain bike brigade. BMX models changed some monikers, and added a few new variations on the theme.

The Peloton was seen just behind the Paramount, and offered many of the same high-level qualities in a slightly less expensive machine. The crux of the Peloton was its frame. It was crafted from tubing that was blended from Columbus SL and SP materials. This enormously rigid tubing was also extremely light in weight, proving to be the perfect mix for the Peloton. This tubing was then double-butted and featured adjustable, forged dropouts.

A pair of Araya ADX-1 700C grey hard-anodized aero-tubular rims held the Clement Super Condor 270gm tires to the pavement. Braking was provided by Dia-Compe NGC 400 alloy, side-pull calipers with drilled and hooded alloy levers.

Frames were finished in Scarlet paint, regardless of which size was purchased; 19-inch (S39), 21-inch (S41), 22-inch (S42), 23-inch (S43) and 25-inch (S45) were listed in the catalog. This combination of lightweight alloys weighed a total of only 22 pounds.

Seen just slightly down the family tree was the new Tempo. It shared many elements of the Super Sport and cost slightly less. The frame was formed from a special mix of Champion Number 2 EXTRA chrome-moly tubing that was double butted, and the seat post lug was investment cast. Tange steel was used for the front fork and the tangs were reinforced. A Shimano RDZ 505 derailleur was used at the crank and a Shimano FDZ206 derailleur was found out back. A pair of Schwinn Sprint 27x1-1/8-inch tires were mounted to Araya 20A 27x 1-inch silver anodized rims. Braking was provided by a pair of Dia-Compe GX 500N alloy side-pull calipers, activated by drilled levers fitted with rubber boots. Frame sizes of 19-inch (S19), 21-inch (S21), 23-inch (S23) and 25-inch (S25) were available in

Champagne or Black. The Tempo weighed only 26 pounds.

The mountain bike segment of the market had not been considered to be long-lived by Schwinn, but they threw their hat into the ring nonetheless. The Sierra had appeared in 1983, so 1984 saw the High Sierra enter the stage. While the Sierra had a few frame tubes drawn from chrome-moly tubing, the High Sierra upped the ante, being built with almost nothing but the ultra light CrMo material. Even the fork tubes were crafted from the 4130 material. In place of the Shimano derailleur, Sun Tour Mountech hardware was used.

The same Dia-Compe 980 braking gear was applied to the High Sierra as was found on the Sierra model. National Panaracer tires were stretched over the rims, and 14-gauge stainless steel spokes held everything in line. Black or Smokey

The silver forks accented the overall color scheme and gave the Schwinn name an obvious home.

The 1981 dealer catalog/calendar showed the Town & Country adult three-wheeler along with their more popular models.

The Paramount name is usually associated with lightweight bikes, but this 1992 model is of the all-terrain variety.

Pearl paint could be selected to cover the 18-inch (HS8), 21-inch (HS1) or 23-inch (HS3) frame the buyer selected.

The Mesa Runner was yet another variation on the mountain bike theme for 1984. Built for either off-road or on-road adventures, its construction consisted of heavier weight materials. Hi-tensile steel replaced the lighter chrome-moly tubing of the Sierra models and most of the components were also of lesser quality. Despite the lack of lighter materials and the top notch hardware, the Mesa Runner weighed nearly the same as the Sierras and cost substantially less. Your choice of 18-inch (MR8) or 21-inch (MR1) frames could be finished in Charcoal or Maroon paint.

The BMX regime for 1984 was altered slightly for the new year, but all models wore new nameplates. The Predator series included the P2600,

P2200 and P2000 models. Gone were the plastic chain guards of 1983, leaving exposed drive chains in their wake. The P2600 wore the same molded wheels, as well as the circular reflectors as seen on the Mag model of 1983, but the frame now lacked the reinforcing plate mounted near the steering head. The "P" models were all sold in chrome finish with your choice of black or blue accents.

The Thrasher series remained, but were now referred to as "T" models. The Thrasher MAG of 1983 was now the T1100, and the Free the T1000. The Manta-Ray had morphed into the T111, and the Mini became the T17. The T130 was seen as a new model, but was merely the MAG-equipped T1100 with spoke wheels.

Although the Manta-Ray had become the T111 in the BMX lineup, it was still known as the Manta-Ray in the Juvenile models class.

The rider had 21 speeds at his command to deliver exactly the right gear for any condition.

Class divisions continued as riders chose specific styles of machines for their lifestyles. Despite Schwinn's earlier dismissal of the trend as a fad, they had jumped in with both feet by 1987. A separate catalog listed nothing but all-terrain models for 1987.

At the top of the mountain was the Paramountain. Built with the same level of care and hand-craftsmanship of the Paramount, this edition was built for off-road use instead of the track. Sold as an assembled frameset only, the Paramountain was geared towards those who wanted their machine to be just that: theirs. Factory options included 17-inch, 18-inch, 19-inch, 20-inch, 21-inch and 22-inch frames and a choice of Cobalt Black, Wild Red or Lazer Yellow paint.

The balance of the "All-Terrain Bicycles" catalog for 1987 featured returning models, including the Cruiser line of balloon tire Schwinns.

The catalog for 1989 models was divided into two segments, all terrain and lightweight. The two halves met in the middle, and the catalog could be opened from either end to view the contents, depending on which bikes drew your interest.

Within the pages of the lightweight side, the Paramount models led the race. The legendary Paramount had led and won numerous races in its 50 years of production, and nothing had yet slowed them down. In 1988, the Schwinn/Wheaties Pro Team recorded more than 40 wins aboard Paramounts.

For 1989, three different tubing options were offered to the buyer. From the beginning, the Paramount provided the serious or professional rider with a custom-tailored machine, and the 1989

Although the front fork was of a simple tubular design, it was fitted with a suspension system to smooth out the ride and protect the rider from some of the shocks.

models carried that tradition into the new year.

The Paramounts with Columbus Tubing were updates for the 1989 model year. The standard Paramount frame was assembled using rifled Columbus SLX tubing imported from Italy. For frames over 570mm (22.5") a mixture of Columbus SL/SP tubing was used for added strength. Each

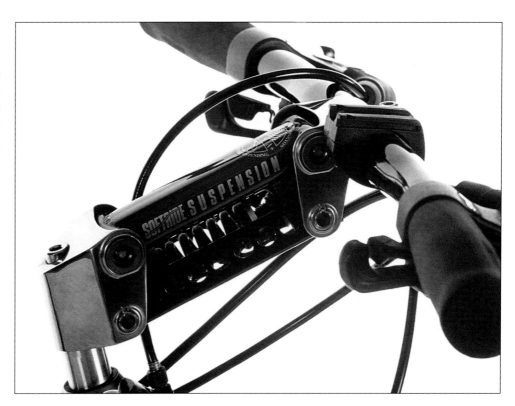

Activated by the double-pivoted skeleton on the outside, the spring within was the core of the Softride suspension mounted to the front of the Paramount.

handcrafted frame was crafted using forged Shimano dropouts and investment cast lugs and bottom bracket for the extra measure of strength.

A short top tube option was offered as well. These frames rode with an increased fork rake due to the shortened tube. The altered rake and top tube required the use of a 26-inch front wheel. These frames were also priced higher than the standard models.

The third choice in the frame was the Paramount made with Paramount tubing. This was considered to be THE elite choice for discerning racers. Its oversized yet thinner-walled tubing was connected using an exclusive lug design of "the exact rigidity for optimum rider efficiency," as Schwinn literature proclaimed.

Frame size choices were nearly endless for these champion machines. The Columbus tube Paramount offered 18-inch, 19-inch, 20-inch and sizes between 21-inch and 25-inch in half-inch

increments. The short top tube variants allowed for 18-inch, 19-inch, 20-inch, 21-inch, 21-1/2-inch, 22-inch, 22-1/2-inch, and 23-inch frames. The Paramount tubed versions began at 21-inch and rolled up to a maximum of 27-inch in dimension.

Bare chassis could also be purchased, allowing the rider to custom build a machine to meet his exacting needs. The Prologue was assembled using hand-brazing and was designed for "road, criterium or training." It was sold in red and white (PL-RT7) or a black and gray scheme (PL-BT7). The Prologue TT was designed with a downward sloping top tube that allowed the use of a 24-inch front wheel. This radical angle positioned the rider for an aggressive aerodynamic stance. Its design lent itself best to time trials and triathlon competitions.

A new line of aluminum-framed models was first seen in 1989, too. The 974, 754 and 564 provided the rider the ultimate choices in an all-aluminum frame. All three models were the ultimate in design and strength, and ran with 14 speeds on tap. In keeping with the custom bike frame of mind, all three versions were offered in a variety of sizes. The 974 ran from 19-inch to 25-inch and was sold in Ice Blue only. Final weight was a scant 20 pounds. The 754 selection included 19-inch, 21-inch, 22-inch, 23-inch and 25-inch frames. It also weighed in at 20 pounds and could be had in Atlantic Blue or White Pearl. The 564 offered only four frame sizes: 19-inch, 21-inch, 23-inch, and 25-inch. It weighed one pound more than the 754 and 974 and offered the choice of black or scarlet paint.

For those people who enjoyed racing in tandem, the Duo Sport offered a raft of racing components as well as comfort for two riders. Eighteen speeds were at their fingertips, and the shifting was delivered via the Suntour Accushift for accuracy and bar-con levers for strength.

Numerous other models were also shown among the lightweights including the Prelude, Circuit, Tempo, Le Tour, Traveler, Voyageur and World Sport. The Sprint, Caliente and World completed the lineup.

In the all terrain department, there was also a wide range of machines to suit every rider's needs and desires.

At the top of the heap was the Project Kom 10. Incorporating radical frame geometries and frames made of Tange Prestige tubing, the Kom 10 left few demands unmet. Eighteen speeds were available to the rider, and shifts were delivered with Shimano Deore XT SIS components. Frame size options ran from 17-inch to 21-inch in one-inch increments.

"Team Issue" red, white and blue paint, complete with factory decals, was protected by a layer of clear coat.

From the extreme Kom 10 to the more subtle Neu-City, Schwinn was doing its best to satisfy all comers. The Neu-City was aimed at the new rider, and provided comfort and fun with 10 speeds and steel wheels in a 33-pound package. The Neu-City was sold in men's and women's varieties, too. Men could choose from 19-inch, 21-inch and 23-inch models while women were offered a single 17-inch frame size. Men rode on Sky Blue and women on Poppy Red.

Many changes in the BMX family were cosmetic or based in the new Series listings of models. Within the Predator Team Series, the Team 24 was a new listing.

A few more traditional choices remained on the roster as well. The Collegiate and World Tourist provided an upright seating position and multiple speeds in a proven format.

The Cantilever Cruiser delivered an extra measure of comfort with the application of bigger rims and tires, additional padding on the saddle and a sturdy frame. A single speed and coaster brake were all you needed for comfortable fun. The Cruiser was assembled around a ladies frame with

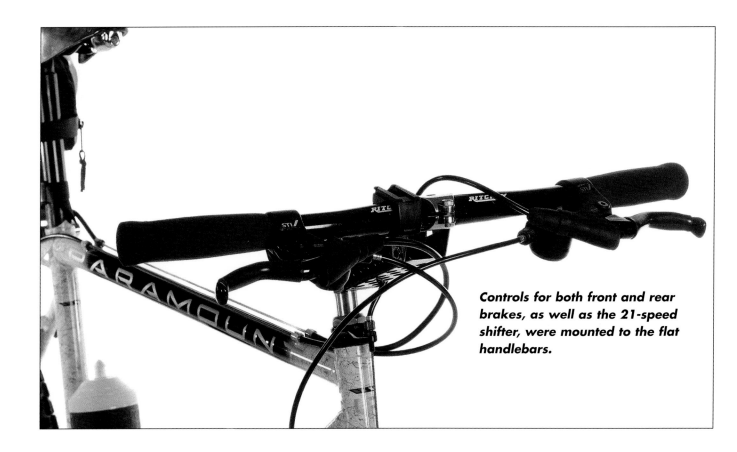

Controls for both front and rear brakes, as well as the 21-speed shifter, were mounted to the flat handlebars.

a lowered top tube for easier access. The 5-Speed Cruiser Supreme added 5-speed gearing with ATB shift levers to the Cruiser frame.

Perched on the precipice of their 1993 bankruptcy filing, Schwinn listed no new models in their 1993 catalog but still offered a wide variety of mounts. Eight off-road, four Cross-Fitness and seven Recreational models filled the environmentally-correct catalog for 1992. A printed statement on the back page extolled the virtues of their recycling efforts, and even the catalog itself was printed on recycled paper and could be recycled itself.

One off-road model shown was the Impact Pro. Finished in a white and black speckled "dalmatian" paint scheme, it offered rugged qualities that the serious rider demanded. A simple all-black version was also an option. The frame was composed of oversize tubing that was butted for strength. Both the stays and front fork were designed to absorb shock, and Ritchey Vantage Sport rims were mated to KOM Katahdin blackwall tires. The 32-inch wheels were of the quick-release nature and sported stainless steel spokes. The Rapid-Fire drive train was finished in black and silver and built by Shimano.

Twenty-one speeds were at the rider's command, and the chrome-moly stem, alloy bars and Tioga Avenger headset were all finished in black. Shimano enter-pull caliper brakes–300LX Linear Response, to be exact–were found on both ends of the chassis.

The Sierra MOS was a near twin to the Impact Pro but carried a few additional upgrades, making it the top of the line. Shimano 400LX derailleurs replaced the 300LX on the Impact. The Sierra also featured 400LX Superglide chainrings. Braking on the Sierra was also improved with the installation of Shimano Deore components.

Chrome-moly bars and enhanced spokes were the final upgrades the Sierra enjoyed over the Impact. Red with Black Spider, or Geo Blue were the hues offered to the Sierra buyer.

Four frame sizes were sold for either model, allowing the rider to choose from 15-inch, 17-inch, 19-inch and 21-inch versions. Both the Sierra MOS and Impact Pro weighed a total of 28 pounds each, proving that durability could be achieved at low weight.

In the Cross/Fitness category, the CrissCross returned after being Schwinn's Number 1 seller in 1991. The True Temper chrome-moly frame delivered terrific handling, and the SunTour, X-Press shifter provided a choice of 21 speeds. Both front and rear hubs were quick-release, allowing for easier transport. Silver-anodized alloy rims held the skin wall Cross tires in place. Guys could choose from 16-inch, 18-inch, 20-inch or 22-inch frames, while women could choose from 17-inch and 19-inch versions. Blue Velvet Gas and Black Emerald were the color options for both men's and women's models. The CrissCross weighed in at an airy 27 pounds, making it a popular choice in 1992.

For the recreational rider, choices included the World Sport, Caliente, Cruiser Coaster, Cruiser Supreme, Suburban and Montague M1000. The Cruiser Supreme offered six-speed gearing over the Cruiser Coaster's single speed, and both variants were sold with men's or lady's frames.

At the top of the mountain was the Paramountain. Built with the same level of care and hand-craftsmanship of the Paramount, this edition was built for off-road use instead of the track.

The Montague M1000 "rides like a mountain bike but carries like a briefcase," Schwinn claimed. The folding Bi-frame permitted the M100 to be stowed in a truck, or be carried into the office after arriving at work. A carrying case was available at extra cost. Even with its convenient folding frame, the M1000 provided eighteen speeds, a quick-release front hub, and a sumptuous padded saddle.

Schwinn

Renewal and Rebirth

Chapter 10

After almost a century of being in the business of making bicycles, the Schwinn company found itself in hot water when 1993 rolled into view. The venerable firm had lost sight of the overall market, missed the initial rush into the mountain bike trend, and was losing the battle against imported models being sold by other makers. They faced only a few options, none of which was pleasant. Their immediate goal was to stay afloat and continue to grow the company. Doing so meant that drastic steps would be required. The subsequent decision was to enter the company into Chapter 11 bankruptcy until they could sort out their finances and market position. September of 1993 was the date of their filing and was hardly a happy day for the icon of American manufacturers. Although it was only to be a short-lived option, it was hardly seen as a positive move.

The Z-Force bikes tested well in consumer forums, but sold poorly once they reached the showroom. They were conceived as Schwinn worked through its Chapter 11 Bankruptcy in 1993.

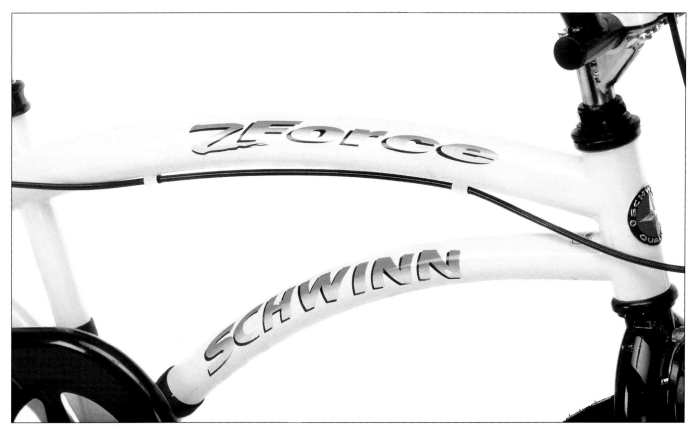

The radical frame design was one of the features that scored well during consumer testing.

One-piece Z-Mag wheels held the studded tires in place and added a racy look to the Z-Force.

No sooner had the bankruptcy announcement been made than things got interesting for Schwinn and its line of creditors waiting for long overdue payments. Vendors were due amounts ranging from a few thousand dollars to the China Bicycle Company who had $9 million in their accounts receivable column. A lot was at stake, and the vultures were beginning to circle the carcass. A variety of restructuring plans was put forth, but none suited the needs of the bankruptcy courts. Upon filing, the Schwinn family was largely left out of any financial benefits, even though it was their ancestors who had created the firm. Many also held the current family members liable for much of the current troubles.

Deals came and went, all without striking the perfect balance between what was needed and what was offered. During this period, other bicycle builders became aware of the potential trouble they could face if the remaining Schwinn assets were absorbed by a larger firm such as China Bicycles. Trek was one such concerned company, and they knew they could afford to maintain their market share with some Schwinn partnerships but would fail quickly with others. They did their best to position themselves for any contingency.

Once the machinations were complete and the fallout had settled, Schwinn was ready to get back to the business of selling bikes. With new parents and a fresh infusion of more than $6 million in cash, fresh designs were being readied for launch.

After the final dealings had been approved and finalized, operations were moved from Chicago to Colorado. The long history of Schwinns being Chicago-built was going by the wayside after nearly 100 years.

One of the newest models from the company would be the Z series, aimed at the youth market, and touted as the next Sting-Ray. It was geared for use on city streets or dirt roads and was built with intensity in mind. It was introduced as a 1994 model at the trade shows late in 1993. First reviews by the target audience offered high praise, but the bikes sold poorly.

Even with the failure of the Z-bike weighing heavy on their books, the reshaped Schwinn began to show a profit in their anniversary year. That same year, 1995, would see a new series of mountain bikes gaining favor with buyers. Priced at $199 to $299 they offered a high level of ruggedness at a competitive price point. With this as their foundation, Schwinn began rolling out higher-priced models to shore up the bottom line. Initially these step-up models were priced between $300 and $700 each, but a premium series would soon see its way into the catalogs.

In order to build a high-end mountain bike, Schwinn need to attain some new technology. They began buying small builders of custom frames, as well as the Yeti company based in Colorado. These radical new frame builders provided Schwinn with the chassis to create the new Homegrown series. These new models retailed for between $1400 to $3800 and featured the latest in bicycle suspension technologies.

Looking as if timing had become their weak point, the moment that Schwinn began toying with higher grade alloys and space age materials for their frames, the market was busy selling similar machines for less than $1000. For all that it offered, the Homegrown was simply too high-priced for the average buyer, and Schwinn needed more than a few high-end buyers to make the program succeed.

The one-piece cast handlebars were both graceful and sturdy.

The Homegrown series was designed for the serious mountain bike rider and carried the equipment and cost to prove it. The "unified rear triangle" frame design and full suspension helped to explain the high selling price of this 1997 Factory Suspension LXT model.

After purchasing several small builders of exotic suspensions, Schwinn was well-equipped to provide serious components on the Homegrown models.

The rear suspension was every bit as advanced as the front and gave the Homegrown a real edge over the competition.

With their focus returning to the youth market, sales in that division began to improve as models based on "low riders" became hot sellers.

1995 would mark the one-hundredth year of production for the Chicago bike builder, and to celebrate the event they created a revamped version of their old standby, the Black Phantom. Only 5000 copies of these machines were minted, and they sold for $3000 each. The high cost was not a deterrent, and they were quickly snapped up by devotees, collectors and celebrities.

Nineteen ninety-five also saw the entrance of the rugged Moab models, and the media was highly impressed with the lengthy list of premium features and the well constructed machines. Seems that Schwinn hadn't missed the mountain bike "fad" after all.

The next year, 1996, saw the return of many models introduced over the past few years. The Homegrown series, new in 1996, was joined by a new series named s[9six] that claimed six models. While the name was rather bizarre, the machines were nicely done.

The s[9six].10 was the top listed model and was formed using a butted, full-aluminum frame with an Isolated Drive Train and Sweet Spot pivot. The series was intended for serious off-road adventures, and the suspension and components reflected that ambition. The front end was suspended by a Rock Shox Judy XC long travel suspension fork. While the rear wheel was controlled by a Fox Alps-4 shock. Shimano LX derailleurs were mated to Grip-Shift SRT-800i shift controls mounted on the handlebars. SunCR-18 double-wall alloy rims were teamed up with Moab Leader/Trail 26îx 1.95î Kevlar bead tires. The s[9six].10 was offered only in Red with a Buffed rear frame section but was sold in 17-inch, 19-inch, 21-inch and 22-inch sizes.

Shimano provided the Deore LX crank and Scott clipless pedals for the Homegrown. They were constructed from heavy-grade materials for the ultimate in rugged dependability.

The derailleur gear was another Shimano Deore XT component and delivered precision shifts, no matter how harsh the conditions.

The alloy butted handlebar system allowed for adjustability, comfort and a variety of hand-holds during an off-road excursion.

VelociRaptor Kevlar Bead 44/50 tires provided the grip required when tackling tough terrain.

The Homegrown XTR was THE highest priced model Schwinn offered in 1997. It featured the best of every component at every location.

A Rock Shox Judy SL, 80mm front fork was assisted by a coil spring and oil cartridge for the ultimate in shock absorption.

The five remaining models in the series were listed as the s[9six].20, s[9six].30, s[9six].1, s[9six].2 and s[9six].3. In typical Schwinn format, each descending model was equipped with lesser hardware to offer buyers plenty of selection at their local dealers.

The 1996 catalog did include a nice three-panel foldout illustrating the company's history. The printed piece had several photographs of early and current machines as well as a few timely facts about the history of the Schwinn bicycle company.

Within four years of the filing, the company had its land legs back, and things were improving dramatically. So much so, in fact, that they decided to purchase the GT Bicycle Company in 1997. This acquisition would allow them additional access to the still expanding BMX and mountain bike segments of the market. Schwinn's 1997 catalog was chock full of new and returning faces as well as tons of factory-generated rhetoric.

Despite the high cost of entry, the Homegrown series was still offered, and the variations were

Both wheels on the XTR were anchored by Shimano XTR V-Brakes for sure and controlled stops.

A Shimano XTR 46/34/24T gearset and Shimano SPD 747 clipless pedals let the rider put the power to the rear wheel.

The handlebars were Yeti Easton Butted and were capped off with Shimano XTR levers and Scott Team alloy bar ends for a positive grip and precise control.

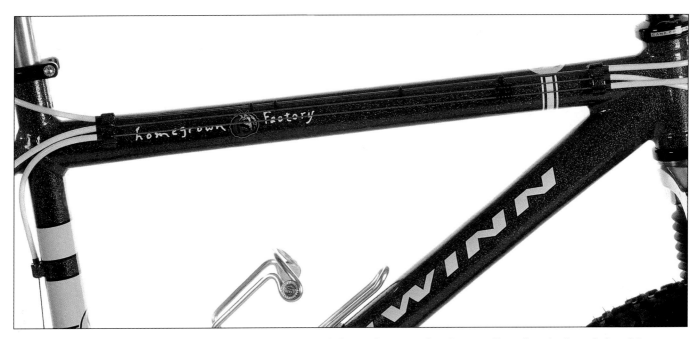

The frame of the XTR was constructed of ride-tuned, butted 6061 aluminum alloy that isolated the drive train and allowed for a pair of water bottles.

nearly endless. Twelve pages of the 1997 catalog were designated to the Homegrown and its numerous iterations. Seven different models could be configured with a variety of frame sizes, and three different raw chassis could be purchased to "grow your own" example.

Leading off the Homegrown parade in 1997 was the Factory Suspension XTR model. This variant was THE one to ride if you were truly serious about your craft. The butted 6061 aluminum alloy frame provided the necessary rigidity for the suspension components at both wheels. The Rock Shox package included a Judy SL fork that delivered a full 80mm of travel. The rear end was fitted with a combination Super Deluxe, spring and oil cartridge shock that allowed for 3-3/4-inch of travel. This unit was adjustable for both compression and rebound damping. The "monster-sized" pivot was part of the suspension scheme.

Shimano XTR components were used extensively, proving that the Homegrown would not be outshone by any other machine. With 24 speeds aboard, you were sure to find just the right one to suit your needs. Mavic 220 alloy rims were complete with double wall construction and fit perfectly to the Tioga Edge 26x1.85-inch Kevlar bead tires. Stainless steel DT Revolution spokes were held in position by alloy nipples.

Frame options were 15-inch, 17-inch, 19-inch and 21-inch with Team Bass Boat Blue and Buffed frame sections being the only choice shown. The XT and LXT models were similar in construction but were assembled using different Shimano gear. Still very well built and fully equipped, they allowed the buyer to trim a few dollars off the price tag.

Four hardtail models were also seen in the 1997 catalog. The XTR was followed by the ESP, XT and LXT variants. The XTR was fitted with all the best components, but like all the hardtail models lacked the rear suspension of the XTR, XT and LXT. The XTR's frame was formed from butted 7005 Easton Elite aluminum, while the rest of the hardtails used

While the standard Mavic alloy rims were light, the addition of these carbon-fiber Spinergy wheels saved a few ounces and provided an extra measure of strength.

butted 6061 aluminum. All four variants could be had in 15-inch, 17-inch, 19-inch or 21-inch frame sizes. The XTR was sold in your choice of Team Bass Boat Blue, Black with Red Darts, or in Killer Tomato Red. The ESP, XT and LXT only had Killer Tomato Red or Buffed to chose from.

Front suspension on the XTR was a Rock Shox Judy SL, 63mm, with spring/MCU and an oil cartridge. The other three models rode on Rock Shox Judy XC Alloy Steerer setups of 63mm, complete with Spring/MCU/Oil cartridge hardware. Being top dog, the XTR was complete with Shimano XTR components in all the key areas, while the others relied on Shimano Deore XT

hardware. The XTR also rolled on Tioga Edge tires with a Kevlar bead while the remaining hardtails had WTB Veloicraptor rubber.

Just beneath the HardTail model were the "S" series. The S-10, S-20 and S-30 all rode on frames that mimicked the Homegrown models, but utilized slightly less exotic hardware. Suspended at both ends, they were the spitting image of the Homegrowns, without the huge price tag. Typical retail prices on the S series was about half of what the Homegrowns commanded. The S series comprised five frame sizes: 15-inch, 17-inch, 19-inch, 21-inch and 23-inch, and they were all crafted from 7005 aluminum alloy.

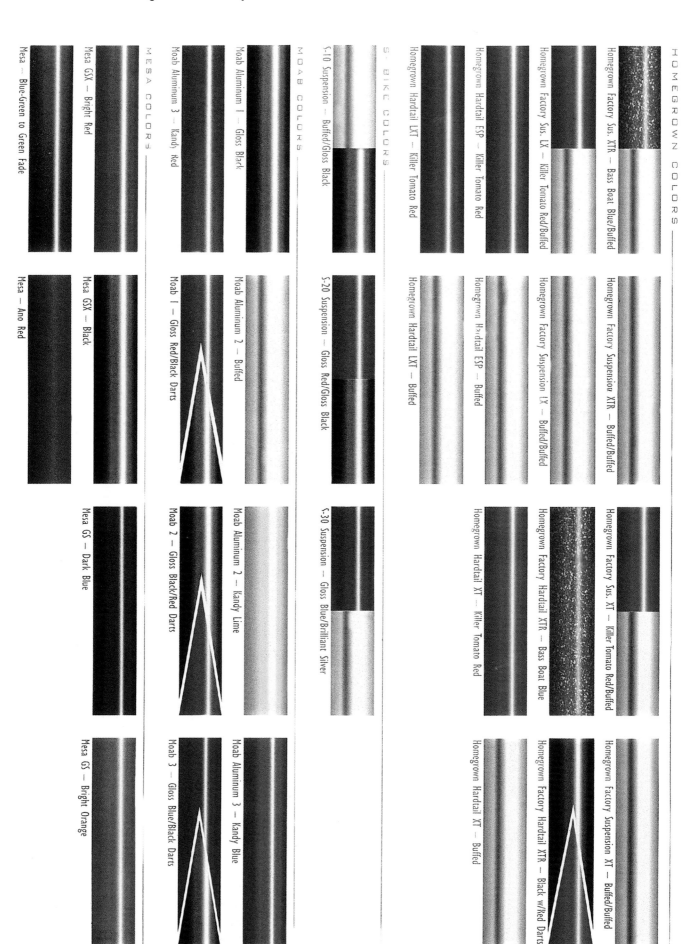

HOMEGROWN COLORS

Homegrown Factory Sus. XTR — Bass Boat Blue/Buffed

Homegrown Factory Sus. LX — Killer Tomato Red/Buffed

Homegrown Hardtail ESP — Killer Tomato Red

Homegrown Hardtail LXT — Killer Tomato Red

S-BIKE COLORS

S-10 Suspension — Buffed/Gloss Black

MOAB COLORS

Moab Aluminum 1 — Gloss Black

Moab Aluminum 3 — Kandy Red

MESA COLORS

Mesa GSX — Bright Red

Mesa — Blue-Green to Green Fade

Homegrown Factory Suspension XTR — Buffed/Buffed

Homegrown Factory Suspension LX — Buffed/Buffed

Homegrown Hardtail ESP — Buffed

Homegrown Hardtail LXT — Buffed

S-20 Suspension — Gloss Red/Gloss Black

Moab Aluminum 2 — Buffed

Moab 1 — Gloss Red/Black Darts

Mesa GSX — Black

Mesa — Ano Red

Homegrown Factory Sus. XT — Killer Tomato Red/Buffed

Homegrown Factory Hardtail XTR — Bass Boat Blue

Homegrown Hardtail XT — Killer Tomato Red

S-30 Suspension — Gloss Blue/Brilliant Silver

Moab Aluminum 2 — Kandy Lime

Moab 2 — Gloss Black/Red Darts

Mesa GS — Dark Blue

Homegrown Factory Suspension XT — Buffed/Buffed

Homegrown Factory Hardtail XTR — Black w/Red Darts

Homegrown Hardtail XT — Buffed

Moab Aluminum 3 — Kandy Blue

Moab 3 — Gloss Blue/Black Darts

Mesa GS — Bright Orange

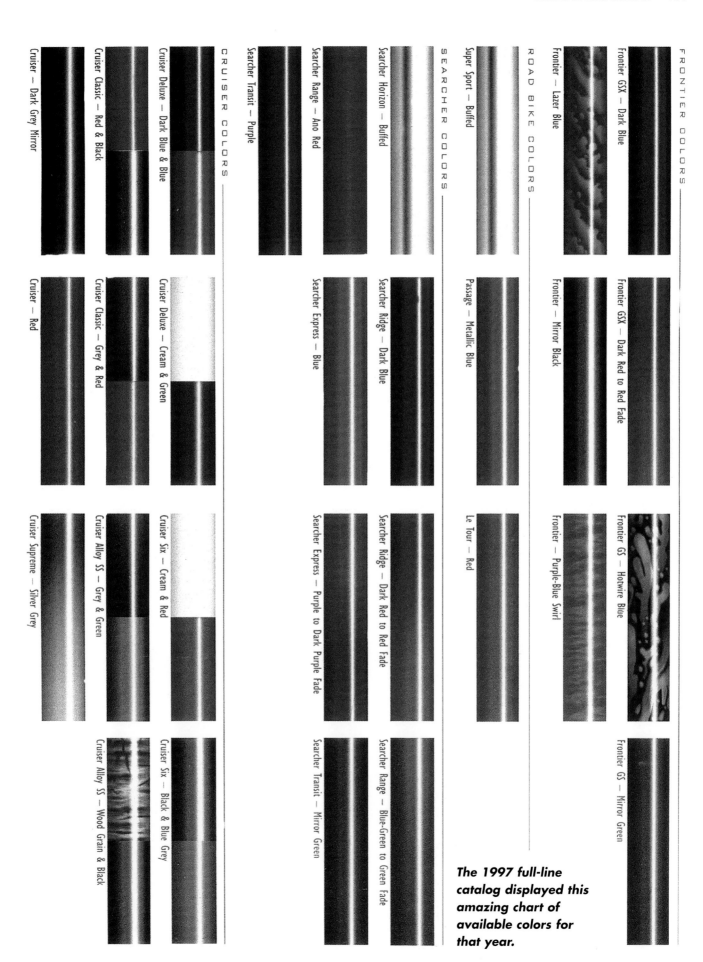

FRONTIER COLORS

Frontier GSX — Dark Blue

Frontier — Lazer Blue

Frontier GSX — Dark Blue

Frontier GSX — Dark Red to Red Fade

Frontier — Mirror Black

Frontier — Purple-Blue Swirl

Frontier GS — Hotwire Blue

Frontier GS — Mirror Green

ROAD BIKE COLORS

Super Sport — Buffed

Passage — Metallic Blue

Le Tour — Red

SEARCHER COLORS

Searcher Horizon — Buffed

Searcher Range — Ano Red

Searcher Transit — Purple

Searcher Ridge — Dark Blue

Searcher Express — Blue

Searcher Ridge — Dark Red to Red Fade

Searcher Express — Purple to Dark Purple Fade

Searcher Range — Blue-Green to Green Fade

Searcher Transit — Mirror Green

CRUISER COLORS

Cruiser — Dark Grey Mirror

Cruiser Classic — Red & Black

Cruiser Deluxe — Dark Blue & Blue

Cruiser Deluxe — Cream & Green

Cruiser Classic — Grey & Red

Cruiser — Red

Cruiser Supreme — Silver Grey

Cruiser Alloy SS — Grey & Green

Cruiser Six — Cream & Red

Cruiser Alloy SS — Wood Grain & Black

Cruiser Six — Black & Blue Grey

The 1997 full-line catalog displayed this amazing chart of available colors for that year.

The Mesa line debuted in 1997 and proved to be a competent machine that sold at a more affordable price than the Homegrown. This Mesa GSX featured not one but two disc brakes to slow the bike when riding on mountainous terrain.

The front fork was from the Rock Shox catalog and delivered competent performance when the going got rough.

The front wheel was slowed by an Avid CPS disc brake, providing both stopping power and control.

Another Avid CPS disc was on duty at the rear wheel, and its six-inch diameter provided plenty of slowing power, especially when combined with the six-inch disc up front.

A Shimano Acera derailleur was in place on the front sprocket and a Shimano Alivio unit was out back, giving the rider a choice of 21 speeds.

The Moab line consisted of six different models. Three of them were built around aluminum frames while the balance featured chrome-moly tubing. The Moab 1, 2 and 3 were each fitted with a different array of Shimano hardware. Moab 1 was the top of the line in this segment and featured Shimano Deore LX and XT drive train components. Moab 1 and Moab 2 were sold in 15-inch, 17-inch, 19-inch and 21-inch frame sizes and the Moab 2 also had a 23-inch version on the charts. Each model came in one color scheme only. Moab 1 wore Red with Black Darts, Moab 2 Black with Red Darts, and Moab 3 Blue with Black Darts. These three models were closely matched and served the mid-grade all terrain rider well.

The Mesa models were new for 1997, and three variations appeared in the catalog. The Mesa was the lowest priced, suspension-equipped model for 1997, but still provided plenty of rugged durability and features. Only the seat tube was chrome-moly leaving the rest of the frame to a lower cost alloy. The RST 161 fork delivered a competent level of control and comfort. Shimano hardware was

evident at all points including the Acera X rear derailleur, Altus brakes and a Tourney crankset. GL-1 alloy brake levers gave the rider plenty of strength when slowing. Red Ano or a Blue/Green fade were the color choices in 1997 for the Mesa.

The Mesa GS and GSX both took incremental steps upward in regard to drive train and braking components. The top of the bunch GSX featured a Rock Shox front fork and a combination of Shimano Alivio, Altus and STX hardware. The GS could be purchased in Dark Blue or Burnt Orange and the GSX in Red or Black.

All three versions were sold in 13-inch, 15-inch, 17-inch, 19-inch, 21-inch and 23-inch frame sizes. "One size fits all" was never in Schwinn's vocabulary.

The Frontier, Frontier GS and Frontier GSX provided a sturdy bicycle devoid of any suspension and allowed entry-level riders to join the all-terrain fun. A varying level of chrome-moly tubing was used on the GS and GSX, but the Frontier settled for simpler alloys for its construction. Shimano drive train and braking bits were also in evidence, but

First released in 1938 as the ultimate in racing bicycles, the Paramount reached its final year of sale 60 years later in 1998.

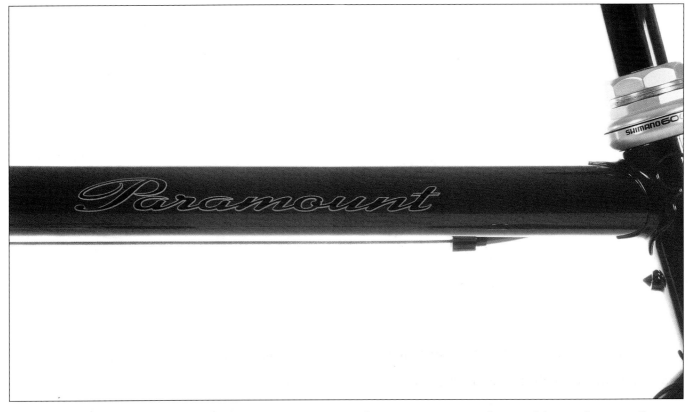

The Schwinn Natural 66 tires were Kevlar enhanced and carried within them 220 psi of air to keep the 700 x 22 composite in top shape.

The "Paramount" script would soon be gone from the catalogs but would forever remain in the memory of Schwinn fans.

each model carried a separate array to meet the price point involved. Unlike the higher priced all-terrain bikes, the Frontier was also sold in a women's frame. The GSX and GS men's bikes were offered in 13-inch, 15-inch, 17-inch, 19-inch, 21-inch and 23-inch inch sizes. The Frontier was also sold in an 11-1/2-inch size. For the ladies, the GS and GSX were built on 16-inch and 19-inch frames, with an 11-1/2-inch also sold in the Frontier model.

For the riders who preferred to keep their wheels on the pavement, Schwinn also displayed a wide array of street machines.

In the "Road" category, the Super Sport, Passage and Le Tour were seen in 1997 sale literature. These three lightweight models were assembled with a variety of raw materials. The Super Sport's frame was constructed from 7005 butted aluminum with forged dropouts. The Passage touted a frame made completely of chrome-moly tubing and also featured forged dropouts. The Le Tour featured a mostly chrome-moly frame but still offered the rider a well-balanced bike that cost a bit less. All three machines were seen in several metric frame sizes. Your choice of 50-, 52-, 54-, 56-, and 60-centimeter options were at your fingertips. As with all of Schwinn's parade, Shimano drive train and other assorted bits were in use on the road-going models.

Schwinn's now legendary Paramount was still on the roster for 1997 but only had one additional entry in the company catalog. The 1997 models were handcrafted with Reynolds 853 alloy and investment cast lugs, much like the original models in 1938. A steel fork was standard, but a carbon version was seen as an option. A frame created by Serotta and made with titanium tubing was also seen for the ultimate in light weight. This titanium frame was mated to the carbon fork, causing quite a stir among Paramount riders and collectors.

Slotted in between the serious all-terrain models and the purebred street machines lay the Searcher series. Available in five different models ranging from the Horizon to the Transit, these bikes offered the rider a well-built machine designed for use on the streets and perhaps a dirt road. Lacking suspension and top-of-the-line brakes, all-terrain riding was not an option when mounted on a Searcher.

Chrome-moly tubing was used in varying degrees ranging from the all-CrMo Horizon to the no-CrMo Transit version. The Horizon was only shown in a men's frame, but 16-inch, 18-inch and

20-inch versions were sold. Buffed was the only color listed. The Ridge, Range, Express and Transit were available in men's and women's versions in a dizzying variety of frame sizes. The Ridge and Express listed 18-inch, 20-inch and 22-inch for men and 16-inch or 19-inch for women. The Range and Transit sold in 16-inch, 18-inch, 20-inch and 22-inch men's and 16-inch or 19-inch women's frames. The Searcher series retailed for less than the Moab but more than the Frontier models.

Even in the complex world of all-terrain and lightweight road-going machines, there were still those riders for whom simplicity and comfort ruled the roost. For this group only the Cruiser models would do.

Five of the six 1997 cruiser models shared the same Schwinn cantilever frame that was drawn up in 1955. The Cruiser Deluxe closely mirrored the fabled Black Phantom of 1949, complete with a

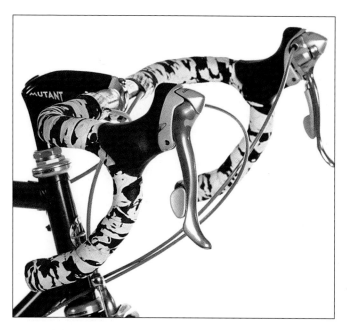

Even the curvaceous shape of the brake levers played a role in making the Paramount the king of racing Schwinns.

In an attempt to rekindle the excitement of the first Krates, this 1998 model was nearly an exact reproduction of the first coaster brake Krates. Government regulations and cost restrictions kept a five-speed variant from becoming a reality.

The chain guard was finished the same as before, and the chosen typeface was identical to the historic models.

The front end still carried the trademark sprung suspension, and just as in the original single speed coaster Krates, there was no drum brake.

chrome accented horn tank and a pair of chrome fenders. The springer fork delivered a comfortable ride while the rider's backside was coddled on the new Schwinn Classic Padded 3-Spring Saddle. The men's 18-inch frame was the only one listed, and the bike could be purchased in a Cream and Green or Dark Blue and Blue scheme. Of course only one speed and a coaster brake were allowed to avoid soiling the Phantom's heritage.

The Cruiser Classic was another kissing cousin of the Phantom, only this version came sans the horn tank and rear carrier. The cantilever frame, chrome fenders and sprung front fork delivered the

A Sting-Ray Slik was still in use, but only a coaster brake was on duty to stop the new Krate.

The classic banana seat was also being pressed into duty, complete with the racing stripe and "S" on the vinyl.

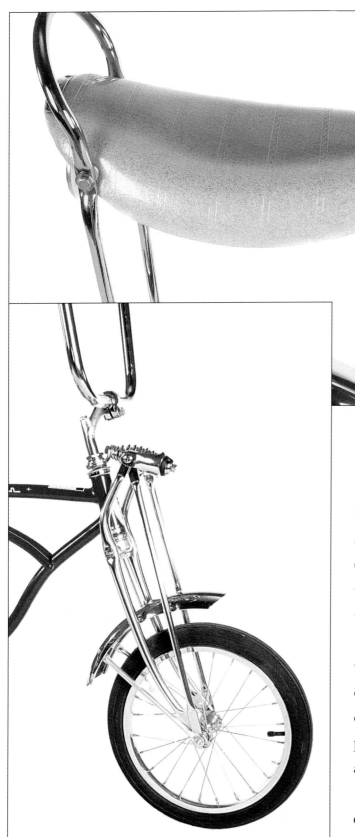

Just as in the original single-speed models, the 1999 Grape Krate sported no front wheel brake but did feature the chrome fender and sprung fork.

The re-released Orange and Apple Krate of 1998 were sold with color-matched saddles, but the '99 Grape Krate came with a white pillion from the factory.

looks while the two-tone paint and 3-spring saddle delivered the past to the present. The Cruiser Classic was sold in an 18-inch men's or 17-inch women's frame and Red/Black or Grey/Red were the hues available.

The Cruiser SS was similar to the Classic, but was fitted with the flat-blade tubular fork in place of the sprung model. Whitewall Cruiser tires were offset by the Wood Grain/Black or Grey/Green paint. Again an 18-inch model was sold to the men and a 17-inch was there for the ladies.

The Cruiser was devoid of fenders, but otherwise shared the layout and intent of the Cruiser SS. The men's 18-inch version was sold in Mirror Gray or all Red while the 17-inch women's model could be had in the all Red finish only.

Schwinn offered 1999 copies of the purple Grape Krate bike in 1999. The modern iteration provided a single speed and a rear wheel coaster brake as did the earlier Krates.

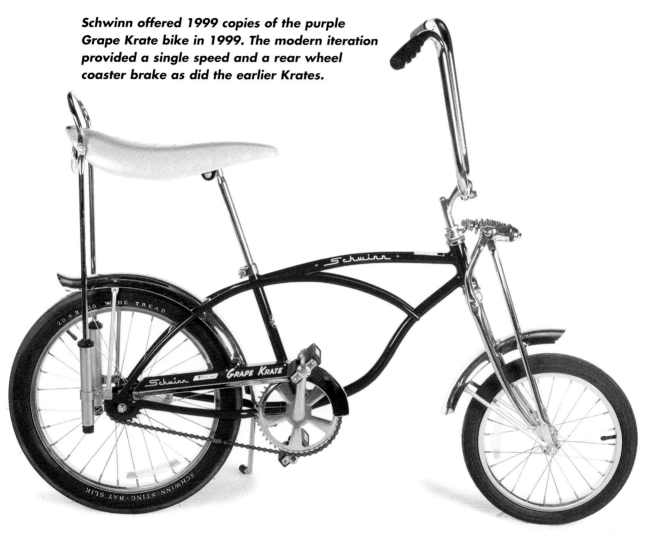

Blue Moon Bikes Ltd

If you desired more than one speed and preferred better brakes, the Cruiser Six was the bike for you. The same cantilever frame lacked fenders, but gained a six-speed Shimano derailleur and a pair of side-pull caliper brakes. Speeds were selected with the MRX-170 Grip Shift mounted on the chrome handlebars. The same 18-inch and 17-inch frames were sold, but the men had a choice between a blue and black or red and cream motif while the ladies were stuck with the red and cream combo only.

Bringing a touch of modern-day to the Cruiser line was the Cruiser Supreme. Schwinn's "Camel Back" frame was resurrected from 1932 and was teamed up with modern components. Six speeds were at the rider's avail, and were chosen with the Grip Shift MRX-170 mechanism. By twisting the hand grips, any of the six speeds was offered up. The Shimano derailleur delivered the chosen gear with ease. Silver was the only color listed, but 17-inch, 20-inch and 22-inch frames were sold to the men, while women had a choice of 17-inch or 20-inch models.

Besides the terrific lineup of current machines being sold in 1997, a large block of vintage Schwinns was also brought to market on April 6.

The Lil Stardust was built around a 16-inch frame made from Hi Ten steel and was aimed at four- to six-year-old riders.

After the bankruptcy filing, the remaining Schwinn family received $2.5 million, plus the collection of vintage bikes and memorabilia. The new owners were more focused on the business at hand and saw no use for the antique bikes. The collection ranged from the one millionth unit built in 1968 (an Orange Krate) to bits and pieces of America's bicycle history. It was a bittersweet day to see so many

Construction is sturdy yet simple, and the training wheels are easy to remove when the rider is ready for two-wheeled fun.

In 1998, Schwinn decided to bring back some of the Krate bikes to rekindle interest in that segment of the market. Since the frame-mounted Stik Shift had been banned by the government in 1973, the new Krates would be single speed, coaster brake models. Just as in the previous single-speed models, the front drum brake was gone on the 1998 editions. Both the Orange Krate and Apple Krate were reborn, and were fairly true to the original models, at least in appearance. Even the saddles were trimmed in the matching orange and red vinyl as they had been on the original models.

In the price department, things had really changed from the Krates of 1968. The new models carried a suggested retail price range of $449.95 to $549.95 each. The 1968 five-speed variants retailed for $86.95 and also carried a front drum brake. Initial sales were brisk, but the production run never sold out. The 1968 models went like wildfire in their first year as well as the next three or four years following.

In 1999, a Grape Krate was sold through dealers. Limited to a run of only 1999 pieces, they are a

great pieces of Schwinn history leave the family that had created them. Most of the collection was purchased and moved to The Bicycle Museum of America, located in New Bremen, Ohio.

Barnard's Schwinn

The Predator Pro .5 CB was a scaled down version of the Predator Pro but delivered many of the same features and qualities as the bigger model.

The front fork was updated for 2004 and delivered added strength as well as more comfort.

The "Bombproof" frame design was built for rugged use, and the side pull rear caliper brought the Predator to a safe, swift halt.

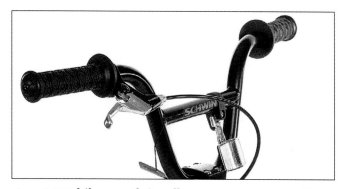

Any BMX bike worth its alloy was equipped with a cross-braced handlebar system, and the Predator Pro .5 CB was no different.

Barnard's Schwinn

Big news from Schwinn in 2004 was the reappearance of the Sting-Ray name on an all-new model. Looking like no Sting-Ray before it, the latest model crossed all kinds of boundaries, and sales would surpass that of the original Krate series in 1968.

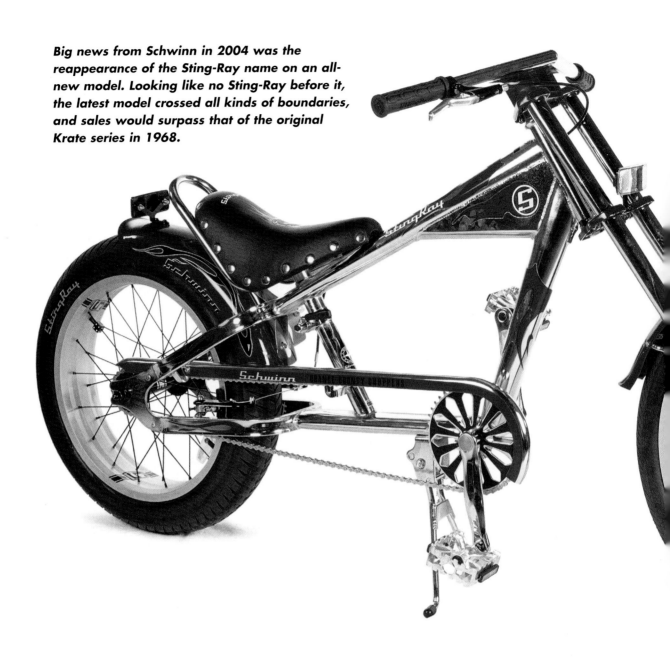

tough item to find today. The purple-framed machine was offered with only a white saddle, not a matching purple version as was used on the 1998 Orange and Apple Krates. A Kool Lemon and Blue Sting-Ray were also offered in 1999, and they were fairly true to the originals. A single speed and a coaster brake were all the latest iteration offered.

2000 would herald the newest frame design from Schwinn, and they were pressed into duty on the Speedster series of Mountain bikes for adults and kids. This frame utilized a monocoque design that was proprietary to Schwinn.

Both the 2.4 FS and 2.4 Speedster featured 24-inch mini mountain frames while the smaller

The massive tubular frame was augmented by a serious triangular brace at the steering head that made a perfect spot for the company crest.

The rear swingarm on the new Sting-Ray looked like something off a full sized motorcycle, which it was supposed to do.

Blue Moon Bikes Ltd.

Speedster 2.0 had a 20-inch frame. The 2.4 FS shifted through 21 gears and was complete with a front fork that was equipped with suspension. The 2.4 used the same 21-speed drive train but had a solid front fork. The smaller 2.0 offered the rider a choice of 7 speeds but no suspension. The 2.4 FS came in Brilliant Silver, the 2.4 could be Chrome Blue or Radiant Baby Blue, and the 2.0 was sold in Radiant Purple or Gloss Black.

The expanded use of new technologies in frame design was evident in the 2001 catalog. The new Fastback frame was constructed using the latest N'Litened Tubing, which was another proprietary item from the halls of Schwinn. The first application of this new frame and material was on the Paramount and Fastback models. The Fastback was no longer a member of the Sting-Ray family but an ultra lightweight road bike intended for serious riders.

"Highway pegs" were installed on the extended front fork, but would more than likely never see use on the superslabs. The front tire measured 24x 2 inches and rolled on alloy rims and black spokes.

The massive rear tire was four inches across and 20 inches in diameter. It also sat on an alloy rim and black spokes.

To prove the lightness of their new frame material, a Paramount was pictured in the 2001 catalog that claimed a total weight of 13.9 pounds! Velomax wheels had been used in the assembly to further reduce mass. The latest iteration of the Paramount was built in "extremely limited quantities" at the Schwinn Epicenter facility in Boulder, CO.

The new Fastback Limited claimed a frame weight of only 2.5 pounds, and the use of other lightweight hardware kept the total number low. The Fastback had 18 speeds on tap and Shimano

Dura-Ace components were used throughout.

The Fastback Factory model was the final model using the Platinum Label tubing that resulted in the scant 2.5 pound frame weight. It also featured 18 speeds, and Shimano Ultegra components were on duty.

The Fastback Pro and Comp used N'Litened Gold Label tubing, and super-butted construction that added a quarter of a pound to the frame weight for a total of 2.75 pounds. Both the Pro and Comp rowed through 18 speeds and Shimano gearing was again the chosen source. Sizes S, M, L and XL were again the sizes available in the Fastback line. The

Limited showed up in Anodized Silver Aluminum, the Factory in Vivid Yellow, the Pro in Matte Black and the Comp in Vivid Red.

The year 2001 also rolled out the new Super Sport series of machines. There were four different levels to choose from. The top of the line SL led to the GLX, GL and base model Super Sport. Double-butted 7005 aluminum alloy was used on every version of the Super Sports as well as Shimano gearing and derailleurs. The SL, GLX and GL gave the rider a choice of 27 gears while the base Super Sport had "only" 24. Sizes S, M, L and XL were listed in the catalog and each level sported its own paint. The SL was done in Metallic Silver, the GLX in Deep Metallic Blue, GL in Deep Mirror Red and the Super in Deep Mirror Green.

Five different versions of the new Rocket 88 mountain bike were also seen in the 2001 lineup. Stage 1, 2, 3 and 4 models, as well as the Disc, were built from Gold Label N'Litened tubing that was super-butted for strength. The latest from Schwinn was the HI/LO 4-Pivot suspension that delivered 88mm of vertical stroke travel. The Disc model stopped by using the two Hayes hydraulic disc brakes and levers. A Shimano 27-speed drivetrain handled the gearing chores on all five entries, but with different levels of advancement. Each model was sold in only one color. Rocket 88 Stage 1 and Disc were available in Matte Black, the Stage 2 in Vivid Yellow, Stage 3 in Mini Flake Silver and Stage 4 in Gloss Red.

All of the Rocket 88s were sold in 15-inch, 17-inch, 19-inch and 21-inch frames.

Business continued to be highly cyclical for Schwinn and in November of 2001, Pacific Cycle bought the combined assets of Schwinn and GT Bicycle for $86 million in cash. Wind Point Partners, an equity firm in Chicago, still owned a controlling interest in Pacific LLC and had done so since 1998.

As of January 13, 2004, Pacific Cycle was owned by Dorel Industries. Based in Montreal, Dorel was an international purveyor of home furnishings and a wide array of products for the juvenile market. Wind Point Partners, the equity investment firm, had owned a controlling share of Pacific Cycle LLC since 1998, and it received a cash payment of $310 million for its stake in Schwinn's parent. Schwinn had no harsh words for Wind Point Partners but praised them for allowing the company to move ahead with their purchase of GT Cycles and Mongoose.

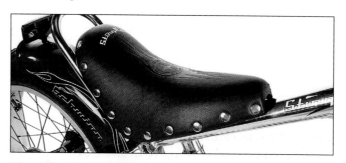

The Sting-Ray saddle was another piece taken right off the motorcycle parts shelf. The chrome studs added an air of toughness.

The V-shaped handlebars force the rider to reach forward to grab the custom molded grips and brake levers.

The Xonex company produced a series of 1/6 scale replicas of the Schwinn Krate bikes in the early '70s. Faithful in every detail, these items have become coveted collector's pieces.

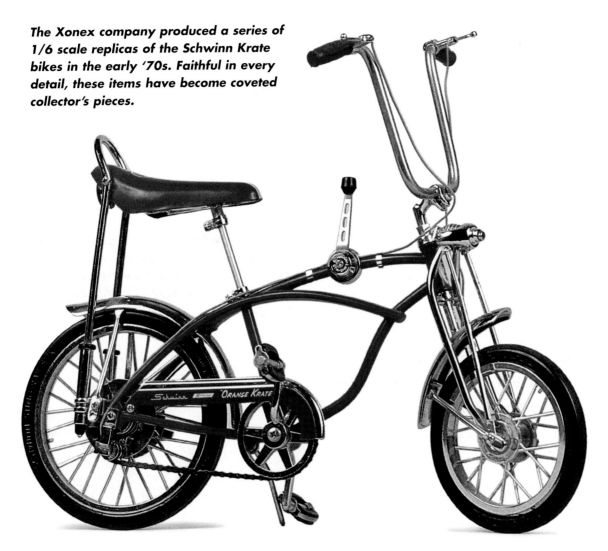

Ronn Pittman

As if having a new corporate parent wasn't enough big news, Schwinn was preparing to introduce an all-new Sting-Ray to the world. Borrowing from the parts bin of some full-sized motorcycles, the new model would bristle with hardware and styling that was never applied to a bike before.

The profile of the 2004 Sting-Ray was long and low, and the rear tire measured four inches across. The 20-inch diameter wheel was finished in a matte aluminum, accented by a Schwinn "S" and racing stripe in black. Black spokes finished off the effect. The front wheel was taller than the rear by two inches, and was 2 inches wide. Black spokes were

also held in place by the matte aluminum rim.

The rear end was complete with the application of a motorcycle-like swing-arm that wrapped around the super-wide, Big Boa rear tire. The frame design was created to mimic a modern day chopper, and the main frame tubes were supported by a gusset at the steering head. V-shaped drag bars were in the house and forced the rider to extend his reach to grab the custom molded grips and brake levers. The black saddle was trimmed with chrome studs to assist in the styling department. A centrally located, wishbone-shaped bike stand folded under the frame when not in use. Front and rear fenders were in place and in keeping with the theme were

MPC jumped on the bandwagon and released this 1/8 scale assembly kit of the Schwinn Continental in '70s.

The Black Phantom was another subject chosen for reproduction by the Xonex corporation. Every attempt was made to capture the essence of the classic Schwinn, right down to the screen printed chain guard.

Impossible to ride unless you're 12" tall, the replica Phantom still looks terrific on a display shelf.

finished with a flamed paint job.

No sooner had word leaked out about the newest Sting-Ray than the fervor was ignited. When the bikes finally hit the retailers they were gone. Sales of this new model exceeded that of the first Orange Krate in 1968, and that is no mean feat. The initial allotment of units was snapped up within weeks, and buyers were eagerly awaiting the second wave of bikes in June of 2004. Carrying a retail price of only $179.95 in one of four color sets, it's little wonder the latest Sting-ray is such a success. Your choice of chrome, red, blue or black frames all came with a healthy dose of flame appliques. Endorsed by Orange County Choppers of TV fame, the chain guard carries their name.

Two more Sting-Rays were also made available in 2004, but as in years past, they were fresh examples of vintage models. The Grey Ghost was first seen for one year only in 1971. The 2004 version would be done in the same Silver Mist hue, with the contrasting black saddle and grips. It would be sold in a single-speed, coaster brake version only. Chrome fenders over both wheels were used, just as

the 1971 models wore.

The second "new" 2004 model would be a standard Sting-ray model, finished in Radiant Coppertone. Devoid of fenders, and having only one speed, the Coppertone model would remind buyers of a simpler time. A coaster brake on the rear wheel would be the only stopping power available.

Thus as of this writing, Schwinn – THE American bicycle company, beloved by millions, its name a household word – looks confidently toward its future by looking confidently…backward.

Ronn Pittman

Bibliography

Arnold, Schwinn & Company. *50 Years of Schwinn Built Bicycles*. Chicago: Arnold, Schwinn & Company, 1945.

Crown, Judith, and Glenn Coleman. *No Hands*. New York: Henry Holt and Company, 1996.

Dzierzak, Lou. *Schwinn*. St. Paul, MN: Motorbooks Int'l, 2002.

Love, William. *Classic Schwinn Bicycles*. St. Paul, MN: Motorbooks Int'l, 2003.

Pridmore, Jay, and Jim Hurd. *Schwinn Bicycles*. St. Paul, MN: Motorbooks Int'l, 2001.